# The Art of Information and Communications Technology for Teachers

## Richard Ager

**David Fulton Publishers**
London

David Fulton Publishers Ltd
The Chiswick Centre, 414 Chiswick High Road, London W4 5TF
www.fultonpublishers.co.uk

First published in Great Britain in 2000 by David Fulton Publishers

Note: The right of Richard Ager to be identified as the author of this work has been asserted by him in accordance with the Copyright, Designs and Patents Act 1988.

David Fulton Publishers is a division of Granada Learning Limited, part of Granada plc.

*British Library Cataloguing in Publication Data*
A catalogue record for this book is available from the British Library.

ISBN 1-85346-622-0

Typeset by Textype Typesetters, Cambridge
Printed and bound in Great Britain

# The Art of Information and Communications Technology for Teachers

# CONTENTS

# To Ann

# Introduction

This book provides a general introduction to the use of ICT in schools, showing how it can be used to enhance teaching and learning strategies. It is aimed at primary and secondary school teachers and trainee teachers, providing a starting point for those who want to include more elements of ICT in their work.

The book is divided into four chapters. The first looks at the general ways in which ICT can enhance teaching and learning. The second looks in detail at the software toolkit that all children, students and teachers will be expected to be familiar with in the next few years. The third chapter looks at the special features of ICT which are appropriate for different phases and subjects in schools. It focuses upon numeracy and literacy, English, mathematics, science, design and technology, geography, history, art and design, modern foreign languages, music, physical education and religious education. As this is a book which aims to provide an introduction to the use of ICT across the curriculum, it does not look at activities appropriate for the teaching of IT syllabuses at Key Stage 4, which is clearly a very specialist area. The final chapter looks at ways in which ICT can enhance the role of the professional teacher, both now and in the future.

All teachers – both primary and secondary – need to be familiar with the contents of Chapter 2. These cover the basic software and the times when it can be used and when it should not be used. Chapter 3 builds upon this for individual subjects. For example, in most subjects students can use word processors to help develop their writing skills, and the World Wide Web can be used in all areas for research, so these ideas are covered in a general way in Chapter 2, leaving Chapter 3 to focus on specific subject-based applications. There is no intention to offer here more than a basic introduction to subject specific applications. Much information and many resources are now available both on the World Wide Web and in more traditional published forms; these will provide ideas which you can develop in your own teaching.

I have deliberately avoided using particular names of software, preferring to talk about general types. For example, although different word processors vary in a number of ways, the reasons for using them to enhance teaching and learning will be the same irrespective of their name. I have also deliberately not included any web site addresses, as these rapidly become out of date. By using a search engine, you will be able to find links to all the web sites mentioned in this book.

I have attempted to create a balance between the simple, straightforward suggestions and some more complex and leading edge activities. If I just described the simpler types of activity, some teachers would quite rightly express concern about low expectations ensuring low results. If I concentrated mainly on the use of computer suites and interactive whiteboards, then some teachers would argue, quite rightly, that without a huge influx of finance they would not be able to use ICT in their classrooms.

Throughout this book I use the words 'children' and 'students' interchangeably. The connotations of the word 'pupil' seem strangely inappropriate when we consider the teaching and learning styles which may develop as a result of the increased use of ICT.

Richard Ager
April 2000

# CHAPTER ONE

# Teaching and Learning with ICT

## Setting the scene

Government initiatives at the beginning of the 21st century are emphasising the vital role which ICT could have in the education of children. Equipment is being funded through the National Grid for Learning (NGfL) and training is being provided for all serving teachers and school librarians through the New Opportunities Fund (NOF) ICT Training Programme.

The emphasis of the NOF training is very specifically on how ICT can enhance the teaching and learning of students in our schools. This is clearly not about teaching teachers how to use word processing, spreadsheet or other software packages. This is very important, because it emphasises that although large numbers of teachers still need training in basic ICT skills, the more important task is to show all teachers the ways in which ICT can actually enhance children's education.

However, I consider that there is a more important strand to this training. For so long teachers have been told that computers are a 'good thing' and that they should use them in their teaching. Governments have put money into schools in an effort to show that in this country we are at the forefront of ICT education. Organisations such as NCET (National Council for Educational Technology) and BECTa (British Education Communications Technology Agency) were set up to identify how computers could be used in schools, and this information was then passed on to teachers through a variety of means, but never in a systematic way. Some schools who had the ability to choose how they used their money spent it on more computers. Government's funding of City Technology Colleges (CTCs) and other specialist schools allowed these institutions to become extremely well equipped with computers, allowing students increased access and an opportunity to develop their ICT capability throughout the curriculum. There was therefore a very wide variation in the facilities and expertise which existed in schools throughout the country.

In industry, funding for hardware could reasonably be expected to be matched by training in the equipment's use. This was certainly not the case in education. Enthusiastic, interested teachers took over the use of computers, but the training opportunities for most staff were severely limited. Some LEAs had extensive training organisations, but these were decimated by the Conservative Government's policies on funding schools during the late 1980s and early 1990s.

Informed by the independent inquiry led by Dennis Stevenson (Stevenson 1997) the Labour government acknowledged, in the late 1990s, that it had to do something to ensure that the huge amount of hardware in schools was used effectively, and to this end the NOF ICT training initiative was born. It was, however, still based on the principle that ICT in schools was advantageous and that most teachers would need to be trained in how to use it. It replicates the original situation where government thought that computers would be a good idea and so Kenneth Baker poured them into schools, effectively saying to teachers 'Now use them!'

As a profession, perhaps teachers need to look at what they want to teach, and how it can most effectively and interestingly be delivered, and then say to government, 'This is what we want to do, and this is what we need in order to be able to do it.' If the teaching profession generally lacks the confidence to do that, it is because they have not been given sufficient information or training to know what might be possible.

And this is where I feel that training in the use of ICT can be so positive to education as we start the 21st century. Teachers will not only have the skills to make use of the ICT tools which are currently available, but they will also have the confidence and knowledge to contribute to an informed debate about how ICT should be used in the future. Governments are unlikely to be spending relatively large amounts of money on ICT in education unless they feel it will them good. I am less convinced that they fully (or even partially) understand the real benefits that ICT can have in education.

So who will understand the benefits? Hopefully, it will be a renewed, confident and knowledgeable teaching profession that will be able to take part in a meaningful dialogue about how ICT can enhance education. They will be fully aware of how it *is* currently being used, they will have a clear understanding of how new developments *could* be used, and most important they will have a clear vision of how ICT *should* be used. They will be able to articulate these views in the appropriate bodies, and perhaps this will lead to future developments being part of an evolutionary process, supported and led by an involved teaching force, rather than a revolution imposed on a teaching profession by a group of people only interested in saying and doing what is necessary to maintain political power. With the launching of the General Teaching Council and the increased importance of professional development, it could be that in the early years of this century, the climate of opinion will enable teachers to have considerably more involvement in teaching and learning developments in school.

## The links between ICT and teaching and learning styles

In the early days of computer development there was a view that eventually computers would replace teachers. This may have been a reason for the scepticism with which many teachers initially viewed computers. However, it quickly became clear that by themselves computers were unable to extend and develop children's education. The fact that computers, or rather the software that runs on them, are able to provide endlessly patient support and feedback to children who are using them, does not mean that large groups of children want to sit in front of a screen for long periods of time. We still need excellent teachers who, by their infectious euthusiasm, make us change the way we think about a subject. It would be impossible to get a computer to undertake this task!

We need, however, to think about what the future might hold.

3

*Sarah passes her swipe card through the reader as she enters school. She sits at a computer terminal, again uses her swipe card, and the computer welcomes her. It then presents her with a list of the tasks that she is still working on. Mathematics is up to date. The daily Independent Learning System (ILS) session has developed her mathematical skills considerably, and she is now working on problems that would normally be undertaken by someone four or five years older. She is, however, a little behind in her history work, and has been booked into a support session with the history teacher at 2 p.m. Next she looks at her returned English work. She listens to the comments made by her teacher as the cursor highlights parts of the work that need improvement. She starts work on it straight away while the feedback is fresh in her mind. After 45 minutes she is happy with it, and sends it back to her teacher for further comment. A message comes up on the screen, reminding her about the group science session which is about to start in the workshop area. Sarah, together with Gareth and Siân who are working at Level 7 in science, attends a motivating demonstration and experimental session with a science teacher. Using a mixture of video, animation and practical activities the teacher demonstrates and explores the three states of matter. The students are questioned, and they contribute willingly to such an exciting and motivating introductory session. They are then told what they need to do before the next science session. The details are already stored on each student's desktop.*

*After lunch it is time for sport, which is followed by a discussion in tutor group about the charity which they feel the school should support in its annual fund raising event. Home time, and then homework. Logging on from home on the free network link, Sarah has the same access to all her notes and materials that she had at school. She works carefully through her tasks. She really wants to go shopping in the morning, so she is determined to get most of her tasks finished in the evening. She looks at the next day's timetable, and notes that her next face-to-face session is at 10.30. She can fit in a quick visit to the shops before that. She completes her evening's work by sending each element to the appropriate teacher. Some of the work is well structured and can be marked automatically overnight by the software. As the teacher logs on in the morning he sees a list of all those who have completed the homework by the deadline and what scores they received. He also finds on screen a summary of the whole group's common misconceptions. This will give him the appropriate starting point for the next lesson.*

*Gareth's friend, Jenny, has been ill for a week or so. Although she needs to rest, there are times in the day when she can switch on her computer, and find out what she is missing. The computer prioritises the pieces of work which she will need to do, combining some, as she will have insufficient time to do everything. She looks at the video of the science presentation which she missed. She is not quite sure about one of the points made, and sends a message to the tutor group's on-line discussion group, asking for some help. By the end of lunchtime, she has received some good wishes and some help as to how she might solve the problem. Towards the end of the day she looks at her task sheet. She is now on track, and by the time she returns to school, she will be well prepared for the next week's experiences.*

All of this, and more, is now technically possible. Compare the scenario with the effect that ICT is currently having in your school.

In what ways could such an approach be seen as more effective than more traditional types of education? For example, do all children learn at a similar rate, or is it just easier to organise learning on the assumption that they do? Are all 12 year olds much more capable than 11 year olds and less so than 13 year olds or is it just easier to assume a close correlation between age and ability? Do all children learn using the same approach or is it only practical to teach in one way at any one time? Do all children require considerable structure in their work, or is it just easier to assume that they all do, and therefore allow for little freedom?

At its heart, it is the quality of the interaction with children and students that determines the quality of the teaching and learning. Consider what learning takes place when a student copies notes from a whiteboard. In the case of most students the answer will be none. Copying, or writing down from dictation, does not need students to relate to the words in any way at all. Some learners, particularly those with good short-term memory, will be able to memorise the words they have written, and reproduce them under test conditions. These will be seen as the successful ones. Others, with poorer memories, will be unable to remember what they once copied and will get lower test results. This style of delivery was developed to utilise earlier technologies. When books were very expensive, and there were no means of reproducing the information within them, copying was the only way to give students their own version of the material. But if they only had a slate to copy the material onto then they would need to memorise the information quickly, before it had to be erased to allow more information to be added. So the teaching and learning methods were matched to the 'technology' that was available.

The relative cheapness of textbooks then led to all students having their own copy, but there was still a need for students to 'do something' in the classroom, and this often meant making their own notes in their exercise books. For some students this consisted of copying out a section of the textbook. Then the technology of photocopiers arrived. In affluent schools, students could now be given notes which the teacher had prepared, so they could be stuck straight into their exercise book (quicker, but in many cases, they would not be read). In less affluent schools, the children would be required to copy the material from the photocopied sheet, as the school could not afford to give each child a copy. The technology had therefore saved the teacher the effort of copying the material onto the board, but had changed little for the students. Questions of cost clearly come into this in that a photocopied sheet for each student costs more than the marker pen to write the material on the whiteboard. But we do need to consider the hidden costs of a teacher's time in writing the material on the board in the first place, and the criminal waste of time involved in children copying it out to no educational benefit. (And yes, I admit that, like you, I have resorted to writing notes on the board when time or some other set of circumstances have conspired to make no other method suitable!)

But even with earlier technologies it is possible to devise interactive activities. If you ask students to look at a series of sentences written down in the wrong order on a sheet of paper and then to cut them out and rearrange them in the correct order, they need to actually read the words and interact with the text if they are to complete the task effectively. At the end, they have a sheet of paper with their notes on, but they have had to do much more work than they would have done if they had merely copied it from the whiteboard. Slight changes to activities can greatly increase the level of interaction.

There is little interaction involved in copying a labelled diagram of a 'Blast Furnace'. Cutting out labels each describing what happens at particular points in a blast furnace and sticking them onto a readily prepared diagram involves more interaction. And reading a passage about the processes involved in a blast furnace and then producing your own labels based on the material which are added to a readily prepared diagram of a blast furnace involves quite a lot of interaction. I am sure that it will already have occurred to you that as the student interaction increases, so does the amount of preparation which you will need to have done prior to the activity.

So, carefully designed activities using a particular technique can encourage effective learning opportunities. Poorly designed activities using the same technique are totally ineffective. Cutting out, when there is no benefit to be gained from cutting out, is a complete waste of time. There must be some challenge – some puzzle involved as the pieces are rearranged.

So what has this got to do with ICT? Well, it is amazing how often students are encouraged to use computerised 'cut and paste' techniques, without adequate thought being given to what can be achieved by doing so. In essence, the ICT skill of 'cutting and pasting' can be compared to a child learning to use a pair of scissors and a glue stick. In the latter case you would start by getting children to do interesting tasks which would involve cutting and sticking. You are unlikely to say 'Cut up this piece of paper into very small pieces – it is good practice for using scissors'. After a relatively short time you would assume that the children were able to use a pair of scissors and glue stick effectively, and from then on the tasks would centre around using the newly developed skills in a natural way, assisting in developing new skills.

Once children have been introduced to the technique of 'cutting and pasting' on a computer, they should soon be encouraged to consider how this skill can help them in the future. Certainly, 'cutting' electronically is much quicker than cutting using a pair of scissors, and pasting on a computer screen can certainly be a lot less messy than using a glue stick. So this means that once the skill has been learned, the actual speed with which elements can be removed and replaced in alternative positions can be extremely fast. Students can now concentrate on the task in hand, thinking about which text matches with which part of the diagram. The thought processes may take just as long, but the actual mechanics of the task can, with practice, be much quicker. So children could be wasting less time on the physical 'cutting and pasting' if they were to do similar activities on a computer. The time that is saved must, however, be used effectively, ensuring either that the student is able to think more deeply about the problem, or that he/she is able to engage in a wider range of activities.

Let's look in more detail at the requirements for preparation in both scenarios. In the traditional example you would provide a diagram of a blast furnace, obtained from a photocopiable resource book, together with some sentences written out separately, which could be cut out. Both sheets would need to be photocopied for each member of the class. In the example utilising ICT you would need to produce one file containing the diagram, and another file with the separate sentences, each contained within a rectangular block. Students would load the files into their computer, and then copy the blocks of text from one file to the appropriate place on the diagram. At the end of the activity, each child could print out their attempt and add it to their record of work. The actual activity would probably be completed more quickly, and the finished product would be presented in a better way. But using the ICT method could also have other advantages. Using the same resources, more able children could be encouraged to add to the fairly limited descriptions by undertaking more research. The same sheet would print out, but it would now have more detailed information included. It would be reasonable to print out the sheet on a colour printer, although you would be unlikely to use a colour photocopier if you were undertaking this task in a more traditional way.

So even in a relatively simple example we can see that there may be advantages in using a computer for this type of task, in particular because it can be undertaken more quickly, it allows for some of the text to be easily and seamlessly edited by students and the finished product will be of a higher standard. Taking into account that the computer costs £1000 and a pair of scissors and glue stick about £2, the cost benefits may not be immediately evident, but this is where you need to consider that the computer is so versatile a tool that it can be used in many other ways too.

In particular, the ability to cut and paste to reorganise text gives students a wonderful tool to assist them when drafting or re-drafting work. Indeed, without a word processor it is a very demotivating and time-consuming task to reorder material that you have written. With one, it is a realistic and appropriate task to ask children (and adults) to undertake.

Once students are familiar with the technique of 'cut and paste' they will be able to use it in many other contexts. They can cut a letter, a word, a sentence or even a whole document, and paste it into another piece of work. They can use the same process to move either parts of or whole images and, in more sophisticated applications, manipulate them in some way before they are pasted into a new location. Using the connected command of 'copy' they can easily duplicate pieces of text, which can then each be edited in a slightly different way. This, for example, means that a piece of text contained in a coloured block could be copied several times, and then the words within each block could be edited. This would ensure that each block was of an identical size and contained the same font type and size, without going to the trouble of carefully measuring identical size blocks – another means of doing tasks faster than might otherwise have been done.

## Ways of using the computer

One of the problems with a computer is that it is so versatile a tool that it is not always easy to know exactly how it is being used. In her paper 'Classroom investigations: exploring and evaluating how IT can support learning', Bridget Somekh (Somekh 1997) identifies three approaches which teachers can take when using computers.

Some view the computer as a *tutor*, with the expectation that a child will sit down in front of the machine and be 'taught' by it, with no further intervention from the teacher until the work is finished. Others view the computer as a *neutral tool* in that children will be able to use it to complete tasks that they may have originally done with a pen and pencil. The task will not have changed, but the tool will have done. Teachers with this view are likely to concentrate on the presentational benefits which a computer can provide. The third group see the computer as a *cognitive tool* which can be used to enhance children's learning by allowing them to do things that are only realistically possible by using a computer. Here we would include activities such as drafting and re-drafting on screen, analysing graphical representations of measurements made by remote sensors and communicating by e-mail with children from across the globe.

As in most simple classifications this is a useful model, but it would be wrong to assume that any one view is the one and only correct approach. My hope would be that in reading this book you will see the immense power of the computer as a cognitive tool, but children will use the computer in all the ways identified above, and perhaps in many other ways. It is likely that Independent Learning Systems will increasingly be used in schools, particularly to cover work on numeracy and literacy. With an ILS, children are provided with questions in an interesting and well presented way on a computer screen, and they have to make a response to the questions. This will almost always entail using both the keyboard and the mouse. Clearly, children will have to develop their ICT skills to at least that level before using these systems. However, using ILSs will not contribute any further to the child's ICT capability. The important issue to bear in mind is that a child sitting in front of a computer and interacting with it is not necessarily developing ICT skills or techniques. In this particular case it is likely that they are developing their mathematical or linguistic abilities quite considerably through their use of a computer.

Once this idea is clear, then you also need to be aware of the nature of some of the material which you might find on CD-ROMs. Many packages, while not being as sophisticated as a full ILS, will provide children with opportunities to practise various mathematical, linguistic and problem solving skills. It is vital that you understand the nature of the material on the CD-ROM and the structure of it, to enable you to make informed decisions about the the learning outcomes that children will achieve as a result of working with particular packages.

It would be naïve to suppose that teachers and children will not want to use the computer to desktop publish posters and worksheets, when previously they would have used pencils, felt-tip pens and typewriters. What is probably most important is that in your planning you realise that there are distinctive ways of using a computer and that you clearly identify the role that it is playing in each particular activity. It is quite likely that while you are getting children to learn how to use a computer they will be involved in more activities which use the computer as a neutral tool, but subsequently, as they become more independent and more capable in their ICT skills and techniques, the role of the computer as a cognitive tool should increase considerably.

## Research that supports the use of ICT in education

Here are brief outlines of two learning theories which are extremely relevant to teaching and learning with ICT.

### Vygotsky

Vygotsky, originally writing in Russian in the 1930s, has some very influential insights into the ways in which children learn, which have vast implications for children and their use of ICT.

Firstly, there is his idea of the 'zone of proximal development' (ZPD). This is 'the distance between the actual developmental level (of the child) as determined through problem solving, and the level of potential development as determined through problem solving under adult guidance or in collaboration with more capable peers'. (Vygotsky 1978)

Imagine a child is working on a mathematical problem by himself. He has a basic understanding relevant to the mathematics involved, but is finding it difficult to progress. A teacher sees that the child is having problems and intervenes, not by telling him what should be his next step, but by a series of skilfully framed questions, leading his thinking on from where he is now, to where he needs to be in order to successfully answer the question. 'Oh, I see', the child says and successfully completes the problem. Nothing very outstanding about that particular scenario. It happens a thousand times a day in schools throughout the world. But let's explore what is happening a little further, in terms of Vygotsky's theory. The child has a grasp of the basic mathematical ideas, but does not understand how to get to the next level of conceptual difficulty which he needs to do in order to solve the problem. Put simplistically, there is a gap in his understanding between where he is, and where he needs to be.

When the teacher comes along and asks the carefully constructed questions, she is supporting his thinking and trying to help him over the gap. In Vygotsky's terms she is providing scaffolding. The 'zone of proximal development' is the size of the gap which can be successfully bridged by the appropriate use of scaffolding. It might be, for example, that the problem which the child is working on is much too conceptually difficult. There may be a whole series of individual stages which he will need to go through, each with its own ZPD, and each needing a whole series of careful questions from the teacher, and he may also need time to consolidate his thinking at each level. Or it might be that the teacher has carefully selected the task to enable the child to succeed in developing the enhanced mathematical understanding required in just one step.

So what implications does this have for ICT? Well, collaborative work between two or three children in front of a computer working on any type of problem solving activity can create an environment in which the children within the group can provide the scaffolding that they each need in order to progress. This clearly has implications for the way in which the group is made up, and does not mean that teacher intervention will not be required to ensure appropriate progress for each member of the group.

But it also has implications for a child working alone in front of a computer using an Independent Learning System (ILS). The management system can ensure that the questions the child is asked are always at an appropriate level for the capability of the child, and can also take the child forward in carefully measured steps, each equivalent to a ZPD. Straightforward questions in a series are answered quickly and correctly so the management system puts in a more difficult question. The child gets this one wrong, so the computer now provides a short tutorial scaffolding the child's thinking. The child now gets the next three questions right, so the system increases the complexity of the activity still further. This time the child gets the answer right, and does the same with the next four questions of equal complexity. This time there was clearly no need for scaffolding – the child was able to leap across the gap herself. The computer itself is now acting as a very patient tutor who is permanently available, and is always measuring the understandings of the child. While we should not take away the importance of human intervention, we should not belittle the power which computers now have to manage learning extremely effectively.

Vygotsky's second idea concerns the vital role which culture and social context have on learning. Again, put simply, learning is a social as well as an individual activity, and what richer environment can there be than a motivating and interactive program to encourage collaborative and meaningful learning between groups of children.

*Gardner*

In *Frames of Mind: The Theory of Multiple Intelligence* (Gardner 1993), Howard Gardner suggested that the traditional measures of intelligence, verbal reasoning tests, mathematics and English failed to take into account other areas of human endeavour. He originally suggested seven intelligences: kinaesthetic, visual-spatial, mathematical-logical, musical, linguistic, interpersonal, intrapersonal, more recently increased to eight by the addition of the naturalist intelligence.

It is probably useful to define these intelligences by describing the attributes which students would demonstrate:

- Linguistic: children would enjoy reading, telling stories, writing poetry and doing crossword puzzles or word searches.
- Logical/mathematical: children would enjoy mathematics and science, with interest in strategy games and experiments.
- Musical: children listen very carefully and often sing to themselves, with an interest in listening to, playing and perhaps composing music.
- Spatial/visual: children think in images, enjoying drawing, building with construction kits and doing jigsaw puzzles.
- Kinaesthetic: children like experiencing things through touch and movement, enjoying dance, sport or practical making activities.

- Interpersonal: children who might well be leaders among their peers, who are good at communicating and can empathise with others.
- Intrapersonal: children who are self-motivated, are aware of their own feelings, but may be shy.
- Naturalist: children who specifically have a great interest in the natural world and more generally have the ability to recognise, classify and identify patterns.

Each person has access to these intelligences but some are likely to be more developed in one person than another. It is also worth realising that if a desirable aim is to develop a wide range of intelligences, rather than the limited linguistic and mathematical/logical ones which have long been seen as important, then children need to be able to work both individually and in groups, they need to communicate and they need to engage in practical activities including working with materials and dancing and sport, none of which necessitates using ICT at all and many of which could not be done through the medium of ICT.

When you identify someone who is very able at mathematics, then perhaps they will find learning about most things in life much easier if it is done in a logical or mathematical way. You would need to capitalise on this, but also encourage the development of other aspects of the child's thinking. It would appear that the task in hand is enormous, the teacher needing to devise different strategies to focus upon different aspects of intelligence for every area of the curriculum. But that is where the power of multimedia computers may be able to assist. It is feasible to write teaching packages focusing on different intelligences. Once we acknowledge that different people learn different things in different ways, and that they can now be encouraged to seek out ways of learning which work for them, the computer has the power to assist in this enormous task. A particular explanation might consist of moving graphic elements, some text and a spoken explanation. Then there might be an interview with a person who was actually there. A whole range of different information in many different forms would allow children to select and make use of the approach which they find most appealing. When planning an activity making use of ICT, have these ideas at the back of your mind.

# Planning for ICT

ICT must be used across the curriculum, in the same way that a pen and pencil are used in most subject areas. What we have now is a much more flexible tool which can greatly enhance the learning experience.

At the moment, most teachers need to think carefully about how they can effectively use ICT because it is something with which they are unfamiliar. Nobody really stops to think how a writing implement can be integrated into a lesson. So while the use of ICT is new it will demand more planning to enable you to consider carefully the objectives behind using such an approach. In a few years' time, it will be used naturally, and the degree of planning required will be reduced considerably. Learning to use any new technique or strategy is difficult. Any change needs to be carefully considered and planned for. A major change such as incorporating new technology into the classroom, which many people feel could revolutionise the way we teach and learn in schools, is bound to be painful.

For your planning to be effective it needs to be based on the feeling that the use of ICT is worthwhile and beneficial. If you do not believe this to be the case, then you will inevitably fail to use ICT effectively. A negative approach focusing only on the lack of equipment, or the fact that the printer never works, will not improve children's learning experience. Neither is a totally uncritical view appropriate. There are many examples of enthusiastic ICT proponents using computers wherever they possibly can, providing students with a very inappropriate learning experience.

In the main is it inappropriate to devise activities which make use of ICT just because they make use of ICT! You are likely to have spent a great deal of time planning a curriculum for your school or subject, based on the National Curriculum. Your first task should be to look at that curriculum and decide which elements of it could make use of ICT in a way that would actually enhance the learning. Elsewhere in this book we look at ways in which learning can and should be enhanced by the judicious use of ICT. At this level of planning however, you do need to consider issues such as software and hardware availability and staff expertise. There will be activities which you can do, and activities which you feel you would like to do, but cannot yet, because you do not have sufficient hardware, or the appropriate program or expertise in working with a particular piece of software. At this stage you therefore need to identify short-term and long-term objectives.

There are an increasing number of places where ideas for ICT activities can be sought. Web sites and a large number of publications, together with many training sessions will provide you and others in your school with ideas for stimulating activities making use of ICT. Make sure the ICT coordinator within the school is aware of your aspirations for future developments. As a school, you need to be in control of the developments, asking suppliers of hardware and software to provide you with what you want, rather than with what they want to give you. Your ICT coordinator should be compiling a list of hardware and software requirements, not based on a wish to have large numbers of the latest machines and the most up-to-date software but on a carefully thought out plan of what is required in order to teach your school's or subject's curriculum effectively.

You next need to consider something over which you do have control, and that is the development of ICT skills from year to year. It is vital that you provide opportunities for students to progress in their use of ICT. This means that consideration needs to be given to the structure of activities which are set. The most commonly used piece of software is a word processor. Children from five years old (and younger) are using them in schools throughout the country, and so are 16 year olds, as well as many adults in the workplace. Is the software package being used differently by these various people? Much anecdotal evidence would suggest that there is not much significant difference. The tasks that students are being set in schools throughout the country require only fairly basic skill levels.

Let me consider my own use of a word processor. I am typing my ideas onto the screen, using a keyboard. I am working with a basic font style and size, which I occasionally alter (using bold or italic and a slightly larger font size) to provide my writing with some structure. I notice a whole series of words underlined in red, and 'right click' on them to find a series of alternative words which I might have intended to type. I choose the correct one by clicking on the list. Every five minutes or so, I save my work (a habit you quickly develop after losing a few hours' work due to a sudden power cut) even though I have set the software to automatically save my work every ten minutes! At the end of a writing session, I will print out the work, and save it to read through at a later date, when I will re-order, delete and add additional scribbles, which I will subsequently incorporate into my electronic version. In order to do this I will make extensive use of the mouse to move the cursor, the arrow keys, and the backspace and delete keys.

There are times in other tasks that I undertake, when I am able to make more extensive use of the word processor's facilities, such as in formatting tables, working with templates and importing a few drawings and photographs, but for my current task, I am using a computer because it is such a powerful drafting tool. The techniques I need for that are the same ones that many five year old children can use.

In order to encourage children to develop expertise in their use of software, we must provide them with activities where it is, of necessity, required. If I had never had the need to produce fairly complex publications, I would never have learned the skills and techniques required to work with desktop publishing packages. If I had not developed the skills, desktop publishing would not be in my repertoire, and therefore I would never be able to choose desktop publishing as an approach to a piece of work. Students need to be aware of many of the possibilities so that they are able to make appropriate choices, and in order to do that, they need to be taught how to use software through carefully designed motivating tasks and in particular, focusing on the software's strengths and weaknesses. These tasks also need to be meaningful in their own right, and so it is appropriate that they cover material from all areas of the curriculum. So the planning for progression in ICT needs to be intimately associated with the planning of the other curriculum subject knowledge and skills.

It would be wrong to believe that using ICT will be without problems. For example, if you identify that spreadsheets would be an effective way to teach a mathematical idea to a Y8 group you need to consider:

- Is sufficient hardware available?
- Do the students know how to use a spreadsheet?

- Do they know how to use the particular features required?
- In what way will the spreadsheet make the learning more effective than your more traditional approach?

It is quite easy to get stopped at the first hurdle. Perhaps there is only one machine in the classroom, so students will have to work in pairs, and it will take much longer for all the class to complete this piece of work. Perhaps the computer room needs to be booked for a lesson, and there isn't a spare slot for several weeks. Perhaps a great deal of time will have to be spent teaching the students how to use the spreadsheet before they can undertake the activity. And perhaps you feel you do not have enough time to spend on this activity, because you have to get through the rest of the syllabus.

Looking on the positive side, perhaps the way in which you were hoping to teach this piece of mathematics would ensure that students understood it far more effectively than any previous group of students had ever done, and this would mean that their mathematical understanding would develop far more quickly, and, with the continued use of a spreadsheet, to a far deeper level of understanding than was previously expected.

And this is really what we are saying about ICT. It is a way in which learning can be undertaken more effectively. Planning must take into account resources that are currently available, but also those which are needed as soon as funding is found. In a National Curriculum that is obviously evolving, there is little point in saying that we cannot teach ICT until we have a room with 30 multimedia computers. On the day when they arrived who would be able to use them? Far better that the curriculum in a school evolves so that staff development and the acquisition of resources and the ability of students to make effective use of them increase by a gradual process rather than a revolutionary one.

There is an anecdote told by Steven Covey in his book *The Seven Habits of Highly Effective People* (Covey 1989) about a lumberjack who is trying to cut down trees in a forest. He is having great difficulty because his saw is getting blunter and blunter. When his boss comes along he observes how long it is taking the lumberjack to cut down each tree, and how exhausted he is. The boss asks why it is taking so long, and the lumberjack replies that the saw has become extremely blunt. When asked why he does not stop to sharpen it, he answers that he does not have the time, because he is so busy cutting down trees! Sometimes, time spent not directly on the task can allow you to shorten the time spent on the task. Learning to use ICT might take you longer initially, but it might save you a lot of time in the long run.

## Assessment

Just as a pen, pencil and ruler are used extensively day in and day out by children in all subjects, computer applications will soon have a similar role. In the same way that much time and effort go into teaching children how to use pens, pencils and rulers early on in their school career, so children now need to be taught how to use a computer as well. However, as the students get older they no longer have lessons on how to use a pencil, although comments might well be made about the illegibility of their writing as shown in subject work. So it is also likely that children will be undertaking tasks in say, geography, during which comments will need to be made about their ICT capability. Your learning objectives for a particular lesson will undoubtedly cover concepts, knowledge and skills related to both geography and ICT. You may or may not decide to share with the children what you hope they will gain from the activity, but there may come a time when it is useful to make it clear that you are looking both for competent ICT skills and sound geographical content.

This becomes particularly important when you give children opportunities for choice. What will you do with the child who never chooses to make use of an ICT application, and only undertakes computer work in focused ICT activities? What do you do with the child who always wants to use the computer and will never, for example, do artwork using paint and paper? This emphasises how important it is for you to be clear about your teaching objectives and the extent to which you will use ICT in achieving them.

Imagine you are teaching children how to use a spreadsheet. You would show them the basic structure, give them some technical terminology such as 'cell' or 'formula', perhaps show them some examples of what they can be used for, and then demonstrate how to build a very simple spreadsheet. You could assess their understanding of that particular lesson in two ways, firstly by giving them a test, or secondly by asking them to make their own simple spreadsheet. The test would be relatively easy to administer and mark, and the children designing their own spreadsheet would probably require help and assistance. But which method would be the most appropriate?

As in many cases with assessment it is much easier to assess the less important aspects of learning. We must avoid the temptation to concentrate on assessing those things that are easy to assess, and missing out things that are much more important. It is also quite easy to assess things that you can see, but much harder to find out what a child has actually learned.

ICT is a tool and as such it must be used appropriately in all the subjects of the curriculum. This does, however, raise problems, as when a child completes a piece of work in, say, history which has utilised ICT skills, what criteria are you going to use to assess it? You can envisage the scenario of a well presented newspaper layout, simulating a newspaper of the 17th Century but containing a great deal of inaccurate historical information. What feedback do you give to the student? You obviously designed the activity to cover objectives from both the ICT and the history National Curriculum documents, so you probably need to give feedback on both elements of the task individually.

It is important to realise that there is much more to ICT than gaining confidence and expertise in handling equipment. We do not develop in children the skills of using a pen solely so that they can make marks on paper. Similarly, the real development in ICT consists of the higher order skills that would be impossible or difficult to develop in any other way. We can select and classify information without a computer, but it can be done much more effectively with the sort and graphics capabilities available with databases. You can interpret and analyse data given to you in a book, but it is a far more realistic situation if you do it with real, up-to-the-minute data available from the WWW. You can explore mathematical relationships on paper, by undertaking large numbers of calculations, but a more extensive exploration can be undertaken by using a spreadsheet. In order to analyse data, you need to be aware of the context in which it was collected and the information that the data can provide you with.

Collecting temperature data manually every five minutes for 24 hours would be impossible logistically, but a computer can be used to do it. Plotting that data onto a graph would be a task far beyond the capability and comprehension of many young children, but by making the computer display the graph you are able to get children to discuss what this line going up and down shows us. And children are able to start thinking about how to relate a line which goes up and down with temperatures which change and with day and night. Above all, as children develop their capability in ICT, the technical skills become less important and the thinking skills become more important.

It is very important that assessment of ICT work is carried out by people with experience of the possibilities of current software packages. A student who has made use of the AutoCorrect feature in a word processor has no greater skill than other students, and their actual knowledge of spelling could be worse than that of anyone else in the class, but the product generated by the computer would be word-perfect. As a teacher, are you aware that this tool has been used? Could this student be seen to be cheating, or are they very intelligently making full use of the power which computer programs are able to deliver?

Let us take a further example. Many computer programs now have 'Wizards', which guide the user step by step through relatively complicated processes. Designing a newsletter using a desktop publishing package would be a typical example. It is an extremely complicated task to design a newsletter from scratch, but by using a Wizard, the layout can be created extremely quickly, and you are also told where to type in your text, and where to import your graphic elements, clip-art and photographs. A student who uses a Wizard follows clear instructions and is constrained by the design that the program allows. A child who does not use a Wizard will be using a considerably wider range of technical and design skills, but it is possible that the finished product will not be of as high a quality. If the teacher is unaware of the two vastly different processes which the children went through, are they likely to assess the two children's work in a meaningful way?

In both of these examples, it is also important to reflect that you would be wishing to assess the content of the work as well as its presentation.

Much of the work which students undertake on a computer is collaborative. In many cases this seems to enhance the learning experience, as children discuss and talk about the issues involved. There will be many times when an activity of this type is not overtly assessed, but what strategies can be used when you do wish to assess children's individual responses within a group activity? Clear teacher observation can achieve much. Asking members of the group themselves to identify the contributions which they have made to the group activity is also a strategy and it could be backed up by teacher records which confirm or disagree with the children's views. Appropriate teacher intervention is also very important. This should not be seen as negative intervention, 'Stop doing that', or critical intervention, 'That's not very good – do it another way', but as supportive and formative intervention, as in: 'That's a good start. Can you see any disadvantages of doing it that way? Have you thought about using this approach which may solve some of your problems?' The responses from individuals to these interventions will give you a good feel for their understanding, and remember that assessment should not be a one-off snapshot, but it should be one small piece of evidence which gradually builds up to give you an overall view of the abilities of the student.

For collaboration to be effective, you will probably need to create groups yourself, rather than letting the children always work in friendship groups. There might be times, for example, when you would like some peer tutoring to take place. This should not be viewed as a waste of time for the child who is doing the tutoring, as it is a good way to consolidate understanding by trying to transmit knowledge to other people. It also needs to be identified as a high profile role, with some limited training given to the children so that they understand that they should not be doing the task for the other child, but assisting and offering useful advice in order to enhance the other child's ICT capability. At other times you may want children of equivalent ability working together on ICT projects, so that they can spark ideas off each other and all move forward together, with appropriate intervention from the teacher.

There are a number of ways of categorising assessment, but a useful way related to ICT is by using the terms formative, diagnostic and summative.

## Formative

Formative assessment is obtaining information about a student's performance which you then use to guide your subsequent teaching. An important feature of formative assessment is that it can be usefully shared with the child so that they are aware of their particular strengths and weaknesses. Sometimes a computer program can provide children with this kind of feedback. Consider a program which gives children a series of problems. When their response is entered into the computer they will either be told, 'Well done, that answer is correct', or if it is wrong they will be told how they might get it right next time. This feedback is formative assessment. It is a particularly positive form of assessment when used in this way, because the program can be (although currently this will not be the case with all such programs) very sophisticated in the amount and nature of the feedback which is given. Sometimes, you as the teacher will undertake the formative assessment. When a child completes a desktop published news-sheet, for example, you are likely to give detailed feedback, some of which may be positive while other elements will identify ways in which you think the work could be improved.

## Diagnostic

Diagnostic assessment is the type of information which increasingly you are able to obtain from ILS systems and baseline assessment programs. The computer logs responses to children's answers, and the number of attempts which they make on each question. The feedback you might get from this would be that all the multiplication questions arc answered very quickly and wrongly, whereas the addition and subtraction questions are being thought about for longer, and the answers are generally correct. This would lead you to think that the child does not know how to do multiplication, or does not understand that it is multiplication that is required in this series of questions. They do not understand so they just give up and go to the next one. You have made your diagnosis and will now talk to the child about their understanding of what is required.

It also occurs when you look very carefully at the work which children produce and usually, through a process of analysing children's mistakes, identify their strengths and particularly weaknesses. For example, you see a piece of word processed work produced by a Y1 child. It is written well, with few mistakes, but contains no upper case letters. You look at the same child's hand-written work and find that she uses upper case letters at the beginning of all sentences. It would appear that this child does not know, or has forgotten about, the 'shift' key. A demonstration to this child will be necessary the next time she uses the computer.

### Summative

Summative assessment is in many ways the least useful in terms of children's learning, but often that element which is seen as most important. The level statements, and external examination results are the most obvious examples of summative assessment. It is categorised by the fact that a wide range of capabilities, skills and knowledge are 'simplified' into a number, letter or level.

## Managing ICT in the classroom

As in most aspects of classroom management there is not just one approach, but part of the skill is selecting the right one to achieve the appropriate learning outcomes, bearing in mind the possible restrictions in terms of both hardware and software. Let us consider a number of different approaches.

### One large screen – whole class

Inevitably there will be times when you want to show students how to use a particular element of a piece of software, or discuss the findings of some data analysis, or share the information found from a particular web site, or perhaps to round up a lesson by doing a quick search on a CD-ROM to find the answer to a question that cropped up during the morning. A large television screen or computer monitor attached to one of the classroom machines makes this an effective method of consolidating information with the whole class.

It is possible to purchase hardware which will enable any television to display information from a computer, although a large computer monitor does provide a clearer image – at a greatly increased cost. LCD projectors which display information from a computer (and usually a video player as well) onto a screen, and which operate quite effectively without blackout, are at the moment very expensive, but none-the-less dropping in price.

### Small groups or pairs – part of class

With the existing ICT provision in many schools this is likely to be the usual situation that needs to be managed. The classroom contains a number of computers, but insufficient for anything like the whole class to be engaged on ICT activity. This is where you need a very clear programme and record keeping system so that you can keep an overview of the progress of each child. Issues to consider include the make-up of each group, which should not be left to chance but should be carefully managed depending upon the nature of the activity. Sometimes you may want an element of peer tutoring, other times you may prefer children of similar abilities working together, and yet again you might want to carefully organise the groups so that they contain children who have different skills to contribute to the specific activity. Another vital element is that your intervention should be an important part of your planning for the activity. You must devise an activity for the rest of the group that will give you opportunities to discuss the ICT work with the children on the computer. By leaving them to get on with their work solely by themselves, you will not encourage them to develop and extend their existing ICT skills.

### Small groups or pairs – whole class

This is the situation you will find yourself in if your school has a room or corridor with a substantial number of computers together in one place. The whole class will be able to engage in similar collaborative activities. This approach will encourage discussion and teamwork and the teacher will spend the time intervening to ensure that each group is making effective progress.

### Individuals – whole class

This will be the model if your school uses ILS, where children normally work individually, using headphones. The computer is very much in control of the child's learning and it is very difficult for a teacher to intervene. It also requires enormous expenditure, in terms of both hardware and software, to enable all the class members to be working on their own computer at the same time. This is unlikely to be a situation that many schools will find themselves in, and it may not even be desirable because of the lack of opportunity for teacher intervention. Increasingly, however, this will be the model where students are free to work on computers when they feel it is appropriate.

*Individuals – part of a class*

This is a more likely model for ILS work, with perhaps half the class sitting in front of computers and the other half being taught, perhaps similar topics but using more traditional methods. This then provides an opportunity for the teacher to discuss problems and issues with the children, many of which could be highlighted by the feedback information provided by the ILS management system.

## Bringing it all together

It is wrong to perceive assessment, recording and reporting and even teaching and learning as clearly delineated activities. They are all integral parts of what goes on in the classroom. Assessment in all its forms should be a natural part of teaching and learning activities. It should arise from current classroom practice and it should build upon children's previous experience.

Let us look at a very much simplified classroom situation in order to see how all the elements interleave together.

As part of a book project each student is asked to produce an illustration relating to a different part of a story. They are encouraged to select clip-art pictures from a reference book and then to import their selected image into a draw program. They also use the program to add additional features to the picture including speech bubbles with text. All the children have used the draw package before and the records show that they all achieved at least partial understanding in all the previous checking points, except for two children who were absent on the last occasion.

The ICT checking points for this activity might be as follows. Is the child able to:

- select an appropriate clip-art image?
- import the image into the draw program?
- include appropriate text in speech bubbles?

The activity is done in pairs, and as there are only two computers available, all the other students are working on related tasks. Of the two students who were away, you know one has a computer at home and works well with her friend who was present at the last session. You decide that they will work as one pair. You decide that the second pair should include the other previously absent student and a very capable ICT student who is competent at peer tutoring.

You talk to the whole class about the activity, reminding them of their previous work with the draw program and then showing on the large TV display screen some of the clip-art pictures that are available on the computer. You talk about the importance of choosing appropriate images for their work.

You set the students working at the computer and ask them to select the clip-art they want from the reference manual. You talk to the rest of the class and get them started on the related activities. You return to the computers and ask for a volunteer to go through the process of importing the clip-art. The student who was absent, but who has a computer at home, volunteers and carefully goes through the whole process with a few minor mistakes which she immediately rectifies. You add additional explanation as she goes through the processes. You are now clear that this child can be recorded as 'fully understanding' the previous draw package activity. You now leave the group for ten minutes, saying that any problems that develop during that time should be attempted to be solved within the group. By doing this you are not letting them flounder for an excessive period of time if they are really stuck, but you are giving them freedom to try and solve their own problems, a vital part of learning, without seeking the much easier route of asking you what to do next.

You now return to each pair and discuss what they have been doing. You comment positively initially, but then identify some ways in which the work could be made better, e.g. 'The colours you have chosen are really bright and stand out very well from the background. One of the people in the picture is very much smaller than the other and as they are supposed to be sisters of similar age, this needs to be changed. You seem to have removed too much of that person's leg as you have been editing the image.' Here is your formative assessment, feeding back to the student in a positive way the issues they need to consider in order to improve the finished product.

Just before the end of the session look at the work produced by the students. With a brief discussion and the pictures in front of you, it will be clear which of the checking points have been achieved, and these can be marked off there and then. You will also have enhanced your knowledge about the four individuals and the level of their ICT competence. You will have noticed, for example, that two of the students were very confident in their manipulation of the picture and quickly achieved some very high quality products. The other two were a little slower in manipulating the picture and had more difficulty in importing the clip-art pictures, but they were supported very well by their two colleagues, and you feel that they will be able to finish the product effectively by themselves later on in the week. You have also been able to receive some initial impressions of the level at which these children are operating in terms of handling information.

CHAPTER TWO

# The Software Toolkit

There is a fairly limited range of software which all teachers need to be able to use, in order to develop students' ICT capability and to enhance their own productivity. The software tools are discussed in this section, identifying the teaching and learning benefits which can be accrued by making use of them. Software of a more specialised nature is discussed, as appropriate, in Chapter 3.

## Word processor

A word processor is probably the most common type of software, its main purpose being to manipulate text. The text needs to be input into the computer, the computer provides a way of reorganising the information and then the text is output, usually to a printer. But why should we encourage children to do this, rather than continuing to use more traditional writing tools? All children are taught to use a pencil and then a pen, but in the past they never went on to learn how to use a typewriter as a matter of course. Why do we now consider that a word processor is a tool which all children should be able to use? It has got a lot more to do with the writing process than with the presentation of the work itself.

It is very easy for written work to be edited as words and phrases can be cut, copied and pasted without having to retype information again. Changes that students make are invisible, so that the student can be confident that no one will know what errors were made initially. There are also techniques of searching for words which might have been used incorrectly and replacing them with the correct one throughout a piece of work. The whole structure of the work can be revised, without having to start again from scratch. Certainly, the material in this book has gone through many processes of reorganisation!

The medium also allows for many opportunities for collaborative work to take place. ICT helps the process of collaborative writing, promoting discussion and review of ideas, document structure, spelling, punctuation and grammar. One student can start some work which others can work on, even independently, at some later stage. Because the information is stored in a file which is relatively easily transportable, the same starting point can be worked upon by many different people. Because it can be saved very easily, there are opportunities for the teacher to look at work at a number of stages in its development, which gives a good opportunity to understand the process that the student went through.

While the technique of providing activity sheets which need to be completed by students in handwriting is familiar, the use of a word processing template, containing titles and the starts of sentences can provide students with a valuable structure to their word processed written work. It also allows for considerable levels of differentiation to be built into a whole-class activity, as the amount of structure which you provide in a template can easily be altered to match different abilities.

Students need to be able to produce textual information in a variety of formats for a range of different audiences. The use of ICT in presentation terms should not, however, overpower the content of what is written, but it is a valuable motivating factor for many students. They should certainly be taught to work with formatting features, but they should also understand that overuse of some features can in fact produce a document which is very difficult to read. It is in fact these 'features' that most students will discover, and use, without any encouragement from teachers.

Appropriate tools such as a spell checker and thesaurus should be introduced to children to extend their writing repertoire. Word processors with vocabulary and grammar checkers can assist language development. It is important that you consider carefully how the extended features of a word processor can develop children's learning. A word processor that underlines incorrectly spelt words, and which, on clicking the mouse button provides a list of alternatives, requires the student to identify which of the list of words they actually wanted to use. They still need to interact with the text, and what the computer provides is a faster mechanism to check on the spelling of a word, as an alternative to using a traditional dictionary. The spell checker will not, however, pick up on correctly spelt words which are not the ones that were intended! Children and students still need to be encouraged to read through their work to pick out such occurrences.

There is, however, a feature on some word processors which allows words often spelt incorrectly to be immediately replaced by a correct spelling. While the program already contains many such words (both the incorrect and correct spelling) it is possible to add your own particular set of words. For example, if you always type in *acommodate* instead of *accommodate* you can set it up so that the computer will always transpose those two words. Now consider the interaction which the student has when typing in *acommodate*. Well, there isn't any. The student can forever type in the word incorrectly, and forever it will be printed out in the right form. They might not even know that they are spelling it incorrectly. So here are two typical tools on a word processor, one of which can be used to enhance a student's spelling through interaction, whereas the other obviously acts invisibly, thus failing to enhance any aspect of learning.

The very fact that redrafting on a computer does not entail starting again from scratch will encourage many children and students to attempt to refine their written work. Minimising the time taken by a mundane task such as re-copying out parts of the material, and maximising the thinking time in terms of selecting a particular word or crafting a phrase so that it sounds as you want it to, is the one overriding advantage of a word processor that makes it so effective.

Students will increasingly be wanting to make use in their own work of text which they have found in other sources. Here again, the power of the word processor can also be its weakness. If students' research leads them to blocks of text on a CD-ROM title or web site, the nature of the software allows them to copy it and to paste it into their own document. So far, there has probably been little interaction with the text (it probably hasn't even been read) and so little, if any, learning has taken place.

The implication of this is that you will need to design the task so that this technique is not appropriate. Perhaps ask a series of very specific questions, so that the text needs to be reworked in order to answer them effectively. Perhaps ask for the material to be written in a particular style, such as in the first person, or as someone who was visiting from another country (or even planet!), so that the mere copying of the information would not be appropriate. We should not, however, be misled into thinking that this is a problem due to ICT. For a long time children's projects have often consisted of pages of writing copied out from books, similarly with little interaction with the text. At least with a computer the raw material can be much more quickly copied, allowing more time for the useful task of shaping, reviewing and working with the text to produce a high quality and well thought out piece of work.

## Other ways of putting information into word processors

We have looked so far at putting in information using the computer keyboard, but other options are available. Children will find that using a mouse – a device for moving a pointer around the screen and for selecting particular options – can save time. This is a vital area of ICT skill development and needs to be introduced to children at a very early age.

With very young children, the use of a traditional keyboard is an inhibiting factor in their use of a word processor. There are, however, a number of alternative approaches. An overlay keyboard consists of a flat flexible sheet which is divided up into small sections. When attached to a computer, the software can recognise which section of the keyboard is being pressed and react in a way which has been programmed into the computer. For example, the sheet on an overlay keyboard might include the words *I, am, four, five, years, old, have, green, blue, brown, fair, red, black, eyes, hair, and, a, boy, girl*. The words can be spread out, so that small fingers can easily push gently on the appropriate space. The keyboard operates in conjunction with a word processor, so that as each area is pressed, that whole word appears on the screen.

On-screen wordbanks again link to a word processing package and expect the child to use a mouse to click onto an appropriate word. This means that the focus is on whole word recognition, rather than the mechanical skills of identifying individual letters that go to make up a word. It also gives children the added motivation of being able to include images, which can either be automatically linked to the text, or placed there manually. An activity of this type obviously requires children to be able to use a mouse effectively, but mouse skills can then be developed in the context of an interesting and meaningful literacy task.

Software is currently available which allows you to speak into a microphone and the words you speak will appear on your word processor. Currently, these systems only work effectively with very fast machines with large memory, and the computer and user have to go through a procedure to teach the computer the way you speak. For this to work, there must be very little background noise – hardly the typical condition for a school classroom! Handwritten words can also be input, and the computer can 'recognise' these and translate them into computerised text. Some word processors can also speak the words and letters that are typed in.

## Spreadsheets

At its simplest a spreadsheet is a method of doing lots of calculations automatically and very quickly. The basic form of the spreadsheet is a series of cells.

Each cell can contain some text, a number or a formula. The point of the program is to manipulate numbers very quickly. For example, located in cell C1 in Figure 2.1 is the equation =(A1*B1).

|   | A | B | C | D |
|---|---|---|---|---|
| 1 |   |   | =(A1*B1) |   |
| 2 |   |   |   |   |

|   | A | B | C | D |
|---|---|---|---|---|
| 1 | 6 | 7 | 42 |   |
| 2 |   |   |   |   |

**Figure 2.1** The structure of a spreadsheet

This actually means 'Take the number in cell A1, multiply it by the number in cell B1 and put the result in cell C1'. As soon as you change the number in one of the cells, all the cells that are linked to it are altered as well. In the trivial example above, this is no great advantage but where more calculations are involved, advantages can be accrued. This links to the other great use of spreadsheets where 'what if?' investigations can easily be carried out.

For example, suppose that a group were planning to set up a charity car washing business. Using a spreadsheet, they would be able to explore the fixed costs, such as buying the sponges and buckets, and the variable costs, such as the car shampoo, and investigate the charges that they should make. If they buy more buckets and sponges, so they can clean more cars at the same time, will they make more or less money for charity? What should they charge? If it is too much, people will not want to use the service, but if it is too cheap, they might not make any money at all. In this simplistic example, the power of a spreadsheet is not really necessary, but it illustrates how a spreadsheet like this would provide a useful financial model.

Because a spreadsheet is a mathematical tool it gives you many opportunities to involve students in identifying mathematical relationships through observing patterns. Because this allows for investigations in a very interactive and visual way it means that many students are likely to be more motivated by this type of activity. By providing a concrete representation of mathematical ideas, it makes it easier for many students to relate to the work. It also means that students are able to experiment with the data, trying out things without it causing long term changes to the data.

There are three basic ways of using a spreadsheet in the classroom. Children can put numbers into a ready prepared spreadsheet and see what answers they get. Secondly, they can change information in a ready prepared spreadsheet, and see what changes occur as a result of their input. Finally, they can be involved in putting the spreadsheet together, including formulas and other programming-type activities. The latter activity is considerably more complex, and will probably be undertaken by much older students.

Typical activities could involve collecting data about children such as height, weight and reach, adding it to a spreadsheet, and then getting the spreadsheet to work out the average, the minimum and the maximum values automatically. Again, you will need to think carefully about the learning that will take place in such an activity. It is quite possible to develop your own spreadsheet which will automatically display the results of the calculations as each child inputs their data. However, if they have not done work using averages before, the number that appears on the spreadsheet is fairly meaningless. To gain most out of such an activity, they need to understand how to work out averages and how to put a formula into a spreadsheet so that it can work out averages. Then they will understand that the reason for using a spreadsheet is the speed with which the calculations can be done, and the way in which as additional data is input, so the average result changes. This leads on to further possible investigations, perhaps looking at how the average is affected by one very large or very small result or how the effects on averages are less obvious as the amount of data increases.

Care must be taken when considering how to make use of spreadsheets because many sophisticated spreadsheets have functions which make them work as a database as well. If you are involved in calculations as the focus of the activity, then you need a spreadsheet.

## Graphics packages

Graphics software is used to create, store and manipulate images. Computer images can be created by 'painting' on the computer screen with a mouse or light pen or by drawing lines and curves at points on the screen. They can also be uploaded from clip-art and graphics libraries, be scanned in or downloaded from a digital camera.

There are generally big differences between painting packages and drawing packages although, as in many other areas of ICT, there is now a tendency for convergence with the latest packages including elements of both types of software.

## Paint packages

A paint package works as if the computer screen is a canvas, and each part of the canvas can be coloured in a different colour. The screen is made up of a number of pieces called pixels, and each pixel can be allocated a different colour. The number of pixels on a screen determines the resolution of the image (its quality) and the amount of memory it takes up. The higher quality the image, the greater the number of pixels and the greater amount of memory the image takes up. You can use a scanner to 'photocopy' an image and to transform it into pixels. If you use a digital camera, again the picture is made up of thousands, and increasingly millions of pixels. This gives you the opportunity to edit pictures electronically. By carefully using the paint package tools you can change the colour of individual pixels to remove 'red eye', to remove something from the background, to change the colour or style of someone's hair, or to remove someone completely from the picture! It would, however, be wrong to suggest that creating good quality effects is a quick process. It requires considerable patience to change fairly small parts of an image, and it would be most wise to regularly save images, using different names, so that you do not have to start from scratch if something goes radically wrong. The reason that images take up so much memory is that information has to be stored about the colour of every pixel. Even if the image was simply a rectangle of yellow, the information would effectively be stored as 'Pixel 1, yellow, pixel 2, yellow, pixel 3 yellow....pixel 1,000,000 yellow'! A fairly typical paint image might take up 600 kilobytes (600,000 bytes) of storage. This means that you could store only two such images on a floppy disc.

## Draw packages

A draw package, however, works in an entirely different way, using mathematical equations to describe individual components of a picture. It also means that drawings are much easier to edit, with individual pieces able to be selected, moved, changed in shape and in colour. And because of the mathematical way in which the information is stored, it can take up considerably less storage space. If again your image was a yellow rectangle, in a drawing package all that would need to be stored is its shape, where the top left hand corner of the shape is located, how large it is and its colour. This information could take up to 100th of the storage space of an equivalent paint picture.

Draw packages can be used when you require a more technical style of drawing. It is much easier to undo errors and to move elements of your design around if you are using one. Some programs have an autoshape function, providing a library of shapes which can be distorted and changed in size, shape and colour as you require. It is often quite easy to include text within each shape. Draw packages have a wide range of pattern fills available and these could be used in any design activity where a range of different textures and patterns is required, such as in textiles work.

Many drawings and cartoons are available in clip-art collections. These are all copyright free and can be included in any document that you wish. Clip-art pictures arc generally draw objects rather than paint objects, so they can be edited using a draw package. This editing should be encouraged. Teachers should beware of children's over reliance on clip-art products and their indiscriminate use. The ease with which images can bc imported into publications should be mediated by an understanding by the students of the appropriateness of their use. There must also be plenty of encouragement for students to create their own original work using paint and draw packages.

An important word of warning is that these packages do not make it easier to draw than when using traditional media – in fact in some cases, particularly when using a mouse to draw with, it is a much more difficult skill. As a teacher you must have very clear ideas about why a child might want to do a drawing using a paint or draw package as opposed to using pencil, crayon, pastel or paint. Use the power of the computer because it is appropriate, not simply because it is there. A child could draw a design using traditional media then scan it into a paint package and by using a series of tools to flip and rotate their own image, design a piece of wrapping paper which can actually be used to wrap up a Christmas present. Avoid situations where you look at an original piece of children's artwork, give the child feedback and then suggest that the child replicates it on the computer. The overriding question you as a teacher must ask is, why am I asking the child to do that? Giving children practice at using a different kind of program is a far from satisfactory answer.

Paint and drawing programs come in many different forms, many of them focusing on making particular tasks much easier. Computer Aided Design (CAD) programs are draw packages which allow different views of the same object to be linked together, sometimes also giving a three-dimensional view of what the finished product would look like. Other specialist draw programs can be used for circuit and printed circuit board design and room layout and planning. There are other specialist paint programs which concentrate on making alterations to existing photographs rather than producing your own drawings.

## Databases

A database is no more than a store of information designed to give a clear structure to that information. Database programs allow you to store, sort and manipulate large amounts of information very quickly. Information-rich CD-ROMs and the World Wide Web are both examples of very large databases. They allow you to use key words to search for and select information on particular topics. In these large databases, data can exist in the form of sounds, video extracts and graphical elements as well as text. The capacity that using databases has in developing research skills is one of their major strengths as a learning tool. However, there are many uses for small databases which children or students can produce in order to store, organise and analyse data.

Consider setting up a database of the types of cars in the school car park. You would need to decide what information you wanted to collect. You might, for example, find out their colour, their make, their registration number and then perhaps their model and engine size. The database you design will be made up of *Fields*, where you store one piece of information about the car, *Records*, which is where all the information about one car is stored (see Figure 2.2) and a *File* which stores all the information about all the cars.

When you set up a database you will need to decide on the data type for each field. This is very important because it affects the way you can analyse the information. If you store information as a text

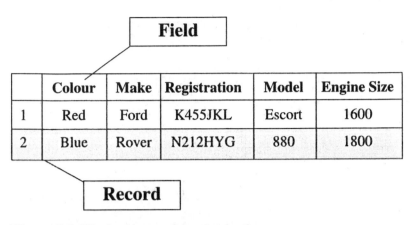

**Figure 2.2** The basic structure of a database

field then that data can be rearranged alphabetically; if you store it as a number field, then you can do calculations with it; if you store it as a date field then it will be automatically formatted to read as a date. In the example above, the registration plate would actually have to be stored as text, as it includes letters as well as numbers. The engine size would need to be stored as a number so that you could find out which car had the biggest engine.

Another point to consider is how you describe the car's colour. In many cases it would be most useful to put cars into already prepared categories, such as red, green, blue, yellow, white, black and other, rather than allowing children to enter alternatives such as light blue, turquoise or diamond white. When you come to analyse the data, it is much easier to do it with a few clearly defined field descriptions than with large numbers of ill-defined ones.

The educational value of databases lies in the way they require children and students to think about how to organise and categorise information, which in turn means they are more able to know what questions to ask in order to extract relevant information from larger databases like CD-ROMs and the World Wide Web. Databases are also a good way of showing students how to represent data patterns and trends in a variety of different graphical forms. By simply putting some data into a database, graphical representations of that data can be rapidly produced. Putting the number of girls and boys in a class into a small table can produce a pie chart like the one in Figure 2.3.

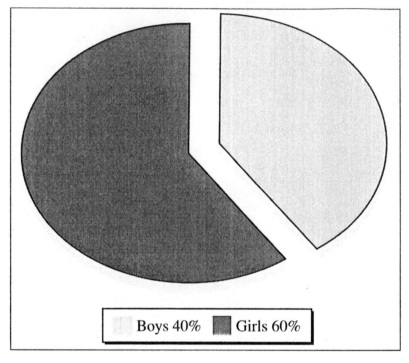

**Figure 2.3** A simple pie chart

Primary school children should be able to add data to a ready prepared database and to display this information in meaningful ways. Later on they should be able to design their own database structure to investigate a particular topic in which they have an interest and to interrogate the database to identify new patterns of information. But in what ways is a database more effective than the same information stored on a piece of paper?

Firstly, there is the ease with which data can be readily transformed into a helpful graphical representation. At a relatively early age children can learn to analyse the meanings of pie and bar charts, long before they have the mathematical or drawing skills to produce them themselves.

Secondly, it is the way in which the information can be easily reorganised so that patterns become more easily identifiable.

Sorting a database of the children in a class first by age and then by height, to see if there is a correlation between the two, is a second's work for a computer but a much longer and boring task for groups of children. Here the computer can eliminate time-consuming activities to allow you to concentrate on higher order learning, asking children to investigate and analyse rather than reorganise and copy.

Thirdly, it is the way in which the computer can search for information very quickly, although it is only when children are using very large databases that this advantage becomes obvious. Looking through a paper database of the class to find out who has got red hair is probably more appropriate than using the searching power of a computer. However, doing the same for the whole school might emphasise the advantage of a computer based approach.

*CD-ROM databases*

A CD-ROM disc is just another way of storing computer data, although it can hold 660 Megabytes compared with a floppy disc which holds 1.4 Megabytes. This huge memory capacity means that it is possible to store large amounts of data, including sound, pictures and video extracts, which take up very large amounts of memory.

But the large amount of information which can be stored on a CD-ROM means that this data, in a wide variety of forms (text, graphics, sound and video) can also be accessed from the disc. Information and encyclopaedia CD-ROMs are actually huge databases which you search to find the information required. It is the development of the CD-ROM which has meant that the visual content of programs has increased and improved considerably. This, in itself, is not necessarily an advantage educationally. Just because there is room to put an 'amusing' and noisy animation onto the beginning of a useful piece of software does not mean that its educational value is enhanced.

With CD-ROMs you have few worries about the information's authenticity, as they will usually have gone through the traditional publishing process. You will, however, have to pay particular attention to two issues.

Firstly, with the increasing high profile use of CD-ROMs as a publishing medium, there have been many examples of material which should have been published as a book, but which is actually published as a CD-ROM title, solely because it is the medium of the moment. A CD-ROM which has a linear structure, and which consists of page after page of text, with a few illustrations, does not justify costing three times as much as the paper version and having to be 'read' by a £1,000 computer. So what you will be looking for is material which makes the most of the medium, offering a meaningful and relevant multimedia experience.

Secondly, you need to consider what form the material on the CD-ROM actually takes. Unfortunately, this is not always as easy as it seems. When purchasing a paper-based resource, an experienced teacher can very quickly get a feel for the material by flicking through, and by studying in detail one or two of the sections. With a CD-ROM this is not so easy, particularly as very few come with detailed written support material. A typical sample would have some specific information, set in a particular scenario, where students are encouraged to join in with some groups of children who are about to embark on an adventure.

By its very nature, accessing the appropriate information to satisfy your teaching objectives will take a great deal longer in this type of material than might be the case in a more traditional style of resource. You therefore need to make a professional decision as to whether the motivational aspects of the style for a particular group of students outweigh the increased length of time that this approach may take, or indeed whether the style of approach means that some useful material becomes less useful, because of what is perceived to be the childish way in which it is put over.

Many CD-ROMs also include games and other activities, some of which may be relevant to the learning which you are trying to encourage while some may not. And then there are the various routes and pathways through the material, which may allow students so much freedom that they completely miss out on the material which you are attempting to cover, as they explore what they perceive to be far more interesting or less arduous routes.

This is not to say that the motivating effect of computer use should not be made use of, but it is important that you realise that it may be necessary for you to direct students to use the material in a very specific way, if the learning objectives you intend to cover are to be achieved. It is not as if it is a skill that you do not already have. When you use print-based material, you might provide students with a specific piece of text and ask them to answer specific questions on it, to reorganise it or to annotate it in a particular way. At other times you may encourage students to develop their research skills in the school library by asking them to address a number of issues, using a carefully selected range of books of suitable reading age and appropriate content. Sometimes, you may set them an activity for homework where the focus is more on giving them freedom to explore a range of different search strategies.

The new technical skills that children need to be taught in the area of databases are those associated with interrogating the data. These should be introduced very early on in primary schools when children are using much smaller databases so that they will be able to use the much larger ones effectively.

Typing in a word to the search engine (a program designed to search for articles containing certain words or groups of words) of a CD-ROM encyclopaedia for example, is likely to give many articles which contain information on that topic. But is a child going to look through all 30 articles to select the most appropriate information, or are they more likely to look through the first few and disregard the later ones? And to be honest, what would you be likely to do? So, in order to ensure that we limit the information we are given and that this is the most relevant to our needs, we need to think carefully about how we encourage children to search for information.

A child, wanting to find out about Ancient Egypt in a current major CD-ROM encyclopaedia, would find 33 items if they typed in 'Egypt' and 36 items if they typed in 'Ancient'. By typing in 'Ancient Egypt' they would get five items, the first one of which is a detailed article, with illustrations about Ancient Egypt. The article on Egypt also has an historical component but the material within it would be less appropriate for younger students. This simple scenario highlights the need for search strategies to be taught to children from very early in their school life.

## *The World Wide Web – the biggest database of all*

Whereas the Internet is the electronic information infrastructure, the World Wide Web (WWW) is the interface and the way in which you are most likely to access information when you are using the Internet. This can be compared to the transmitter and aerial, or cable and satellite infrastructure for television, compared with the interface of BBC1 or Sky Sport which allows you to make sense of the information provided. The World Wide Web is a vast source of relevant and up-to-date material that can enliven teaching in all subjects. Unfortunately, it also contains a great deal of irrelevant and false information and much of it is at a level inappropriate for the age or ability of the students you are working with. Consider a non-technological situation. You would be unlikely to think it useful for a class of 15 year olds to spend a couple of hours in the British Library to research a particular topic. They would, however, gain much from a similar time being spent in the school library where the books and other resources have been carefully selected for their content and appropriateness. Without some structure, searching for information on the Internet can be an extremely futile and frustrating experience. But if you just provide your students with the web sites to look at, then they might just as well not be accessing the WWW at all, but be reading the material that you could already have printed out. As web sites can respond to change much more quickly than material published as written text, it follows that they are likely to be up-to-date, topical and relevant to students' interests and needs. However, simply using the WWW will not in itself enhance teaching and learning – the educational benefits will depend on how teachers use the infrastructure.

Searching the WWW is easy – searching it effectively is much harder. It is, however, a vital skill with the number of available pages on the WWW doubling every four months. If you are going to search effectively you need help from some of the tools which are available on the web itself. The basic procedure, however, is the same as with any other database.

Search engines allow the user to enter keywords which are then looked for in a database. The search engine retrieves WWW documents from its database that contain the keywords entered by the searcher. It is important to note that when you are using a search engine you are not searching the WWW 'live', as it exists at this very moment. Rather, you are searching a fixed database that has been compiled some time previously. It may take several months for new websites to be added to a search engine. Information is readily available about suitable search engines in a wide range of publications. One you could try first would be the UK version of AltaVista.

You should make use of a search engine when you are looking for a particular named site and when you have a fairly narrow topic which you want to research. Using a search engine will mean that it searches through the full text of several millions of pages for the one word selected. Meta search engines allow the user to search several search engines simultaneously, using a single interface. These are very fast, and will inevitably provide you with an even longer list of sites which may be of use to you. But you may not have time to evaluate them all!

Subject directories include resources which have been selected by 'real people' and categorised into topic areas. There are times when this might be the most appropriate tool to use, particularly when you are researching into a broad area, or you want some sites which are effectively recommended as being useful for a particular topic. Increasingly, these types of tool are converging, so that in the near future all aspects of searching through the web are likely to be undertaken from one site. Yahoo is an example of a web subject directory.

If you are likely to want to repeat a search at a later date, add a bookmark to your current search results. This means you can just click onto the website address, rather than typing it in again. It is just like putting a number into a telephone's memory. Each search engine has its own particular syntax to use when asking questions. Typically, however, if you put the search word in inverted commas, only articles containing that string of letters will be identified. (Putting 'New Zealand' in inverted commas will not pick up sites with only 'New' in them, for example).

You should stress to students how important effective searching strategies are to ensure that they do not waste time looking through irrelevant information. A good introduction to a topic would be a class or group discussion, identifying appropriate keywords, perhaps with a teacher demonstration on a large monitor, showing the results of each search.

## Software to help you communicate

There is an increasing range of software products whose main function is to enhance communication of ideas by focusing on presentation. These range from the paper-based desktop publishing packages, through the screen-based presentation and multimedia authoring packages, to the web-page authoring software.

*Desktop publishing*

Desktop publishing programs allow you to manipulate text, graphic elements (lines, shading, boxes), drawings and photographs and arrange them on a page with the aim of producing a well-designed piece of work. As the range of facilities within traditional word processing programs has increased, they are able to do many of the things which purpose designed desktop publishing packages can do. However, DTP does involve a different way of working and it is therefore this process which would be the main teaching outcome when deciding to introduce children to a desktop publishing program.

You should really think of desktop publishing as a page layout package. Imagine you have a sheet of paper on which you want to create a small news-sheet. The sheet might well have a large title, a logo, a photograph, and two blocks of text. You have all these elements available, so you would cut them out and then paste them in position onto your sheet of paper – the original cut and paste method. But then you discover that the way you have typed in your text does not quite fit, and the photograph is slightly too large. This is where the power of a desktop publishing package comes in. If the text and photograph are stored electronically and are placed on the electronic sheet of paper within the DTP package then it is very easy to make the photograph slightly smaller and to decrease the size of the text (font size), or the space between lines of text (leading) so that all the words fit in.

The other major benefit of desktop publishing is the ability to link text from one page to another. Newspapers often start a story on page one and then continue it on some other page. One way to do this would be to cut your article in two, pasting the first part on page one and the second part on page four. But as you come to rearrange the front page you notice that now there is actually room for a bit more of the text. Therefore you need to go to page four, cutting a bit off the page and pasting it back on page one. Did you take the right amount, or are you still a little short? The power of desktop publishing allows you to link the text from page one to four automatically, using text frames. The text is stored on the page in a text frame. If you make the text frame slightly smaller, less text is shown on the page, but the text has not disappeared – it is stored. When you return to page four, you find the text in place once more.

Most desktop publishing packages now come with a wide range of suggested layouts – you just have to import the text and pictures. While this makes the process of designing a flyer much easier, it does lead to standardised products, and allows for little creativity. If you were designing an activity to allow students to develop their ICT capability, one making excessive use of wizards or templates would be inappropriate.

Many word processors are now so sophisticated that they allow for columns, integration of graphics and other features that were originally only found on specialised desktop publishing software. This means that for many applications, the most appropriate choice will be the piece of software with which you, or your students, are most familiar. As soon as you want to incorporate a lot of images, you should use a desktop publishing package.

So when would you want to use this approach, and when would you want to use it with your students? Well, it can make it easier to produce high quality material, although just because you are using ICT does not mean it will automatically be presented in a better way than it would be using a traditional approach. It will generally take a longer time to produce, at least initially, and so this must be taken into account both for you as a teacher, and for students when they are working on this type of work.

Therefore, if you consider that the student's interaction with the work using ICT will enhance the learning experience then it is a useful approach. Similarly, if you believe that the time spent in you producing a high quality presentation (perhaps shared with colleagues throughout the school or department) will make the student's learning experience more effective, then that is the time to use this strategy.

### Presentation software

Presentation software is designed to make it easy to produce overhead transparency slides to illustrate any particular presentation that you or your students may be making. But there are many forms which these slides could take including black and white or colour transparency for an OHP or a computer-based presentation using either a graphics tablet placed on an OHP or an LCD projector. It is important to realise that there are going to be times when each of these is appropriate, and no one approach is the best.

A heavily text based presentation with no opportunities for use of relevant graphics could well be produced as a black and white transparency. The advantage of using a presentation package for the production of this type of material would be the use of a template which would ensure that title and bullet list arrangements on the screen would be consistent, with the same positioning, font type and size and spacing. However, for a product of this type, a word processor would probably be just as adequate.

By using colour slides, you are likely to be able to make the presentation more visually interesting because you can include relevant colour illustrations to supplement the text. These will take longer to produce, but you will probably feel that you are achieving a more polished and professional product. Colour photographs can be displayed quite effectively and judicious use of relevant clip-art can make this type of material more memorable. Colour photographs can be converted into a graphics file by using a scanner or, if you use a digital camera, colour images can quickly be downloaded from the camera straight into your presentation package. Black and white and colour handouts can quickly be produced from the original slides, and can provide a useful learning structure for students. Obviously, colour handouts will be more expensive, but they might enhance the learning experience.

And finally we come to using the presentation software 'live' by connecting it to a graphics tablet on an OHP or an LCD projector. Graphics tablets (and now lap top computer screens which are detachable and which fit onto an OHP) were the first and reasonably affordable ways of enabling 'live' computer presentations. The disadvantage of these is the need for a very bright OHP (which is very expensive) and in most cases near total blackout, if you are presenting to a group larger than five. LCD projectors are much more expensive (although their price is decreasing rapidly) but provide a much brighter and clearer image and can be used in rooms without total blackout.

But surely there must be a reason why you would use £4,000 worth of equipment instead of a few sheets of acetate and a fairly standard OHP? Time is certainly a consideration as you do not have to wait for pages to print out, and you also have the advantage of immediacy because an error or an up-to-date fact can be typed in and projected instantaneously. But certainly, the nature of the content must also affect your choice. By using the power of a piece of presentation software you can animate elements of the material as well as incorporating sound and video into it. As with most things there are advantages and disadvantages of this approach. To produce an effective presentation is very time-consuming. By using the facilities which the software includes such as templates you can quickly produce a very standard presentation which looks the same as most other ones you will have seen. The bullet points flying in one by one linked to some 'interesting' but probably totally irrelevant sound is not the most effective or creative use of software of this type.

Both teachers and students should think very carefully about the reason for the use of such effects. By using the program in a very creative way (and not using the wizards or templates) you can produce memorable and interesting presentations which actually do enhance the learning experiences of your students. The time taken to produce such high quality products can be compensated for in other ways. Perhaps as a school or department you could plan out the presentations you need, and then each member of staff takes responsibility for producing one. Increasingly, you will find people who are happy to share their material via the web, and so with a little customisation you will be able to produce good quality material quite quickly. After all, in terms of presentation, we are all used to seeing products of the highest quality on television, in publications and on computers. Why should our students see anything less than this quality in the presentations which are done for them?

## Multimedia authoring

A development of presentation software is multimedia authoring software, which allows you to produce material which is viewed on a computer and which enables the user to interact with it. This is a relatively new and rapidly developing area of ICT. It has been brought about because of the rapid advances in facilities which are now readily available on computers – a sound card, a CD-ROM (or even DVD) drive, a high resolution screen, fast processing of information and large storage devices, and because a great deal of the multimedia material which is currently available on CD-ROM and the WWW has provided us with examples of what we ourselves could perhaps produce.

Multimedia authoring can really be thought of as an extension to desktop publishing or using presentation software – producing screen-based information as opposed to paper based material and hence using the sound and moving image facilities that the computer affords us. It also allows for greater flexibility in structuring written material. If you look through a book, you are likely to start at the beginning and read through to the end. If you find information which you feel is irrelevant you can skip through those pages, but you are still taking very much a linear approach.

With this sort of program your document can have a branching rather than linear structure. Having digested a screen-full of information, you may be given a choice of routes to follow. By clicking on one of a number of buttons, you are in control. You do not have to skim through pages of material that you know is irrelevant – you, in fact, never see them.

The audience is an important feature of any writing, but in multimedia, when there is also the requirement for the reader to have access to an expensive computer, it is even more important. If the material is designed for a reception age child, have they got the technical skills to work their way through the material? If it is for parents, how can they be sure that they will actually be able to access it?

A typical multimedia screen would consist of a background, a photograph or drawing, and an area of the screen identified as a 'button' which when clicked with the mouse will reveal further information. The page also requires navigation controls to allow the user to move from one page to the next, return to previous pages if they wish or to leave the program completely. Multimedia authoring also gives many opportunities for children's work to be used subsequently as background research by other groups of children, emphasising the relevance of the activity – the package will actually be used.

Once you want information of this nature to be available to children and students throughout the school, the best way of doing it will be to have a school Intranet, where material can easily be looked at from any of the networked machines in the school. An Intranet is the same as the Internet, but for a very restricted audience, in this case, within a school. If, however, you want parents and students at home to be able to access this material, then you will need to develop your own school web site.

*Web authoring*

Although producing web pages is not a particularly common school activity at the moment, it rapidly will become something that students can do. Most web authoring software allows you to produce the basic web pages quite easily. This is a very similar process to multimedia authoring. It allows children to distribute their work to a potential massive world-wide audience, and care must therefore be taken to ensure that only material with which the school is happy to link its name is included. While children should obviously be able to produce their own web pages, there must be a clear procedure set up for checking the material before it is made available on the World Wide Web.

In educational terms again you need to consider what benefits will accrue from such an activity. By allowing students in your school to publish material which is accessible to the whole world, you are giving them the opportunity to write for a real audience, and this inevitably has motivating effects. The Tesco SchoolNet 2000 project which encouraged children and students to produce material for publication on a special web site showed that there was real enthusiasm for such activity. It also showed that web sites could be automated so that the technical issues of putting material on the web were largely removed from the students. They just had to copy their work onto a space on the Tesco SchoolNet 2000 site, and after approval by the teacher, it was published. Much of the work being undertaken as part of the NGfL (National Grid for Learning) project is looking at the educational advantages of distributing material over the web. This means that in order to do this teachers and students will increasingly not have to learn how to use web authoring software, but will be able to incorporate their work almost seamlessly into web site structures.

*E-mail, newsgroups and chat rooms*

Shortly, all children and students will have their own e-mail address through their school, although many students will already have one from their own home-based computer. Managing this efficiently, and harnessing its use so that it enhances teaching and learning is going to be a substantial task. There are web sites which give you the details of schools who wish to communicate with other schools by e-mail. The ease with which e-mails can be sent means that it is very difficult to check all e-mail material before it is sent to ensure it contains appropriate content and language. Software exists which searches for text strings in e-mails that match swear words and other undesirable language, and blanks out the offending item, although this is not a foolproof solution. A student using such a system while doing some legitimate research into the author of Oliver Twist was bemused to see all e-mail references to him written as 'Charles ****ens'! Children's and students' use of e-mail needs to be very carefully structured if it is going to enhance any aspect of learning.

Newsgroups allow students to receive e-mails from all over the world from students who are interested in particular issues. Newsgroups exist for almost any subject you can think of. Some are moderated, which means that someone is responsible for checking that all the messages are appropriate, and ensures that participants who do use bad language, or discuss inappropriate topics, lose access to the group. The vast majority of newsgroups will not have a moderator, and are totally self managed. It would seem incredibly unwise to give students access to these world-wide newsgroups at the present time. Moderated newsgroups, designed specifically for children and students will be available over the NGfL and through other educational sites, and these will be designed to enhance aspects of learning. These are likely to be much safer environments.

Chat rooms exist on the Internet to provide opportunities to chat, in the same way that you might walk into a room and start talking to the people in there. Most of the chat is done electronically, but the intention is that you can have conversations by typing in comments, and then waiting for someone to respond. These can be extremely undesirable places as you have no idea about the nature of the other people with whom you are corresponding. Clearly, if anyone gives out any personal details, they might be in considerable danger. Again, it is likely that educational Internet service providers may set up moderated chat rooms for particular projects, which might include adequate safeguards. However, there are so many other uses of the Internet that chat rooms and probably newsgroups are best avoided.

## Sound packages

There are very many sophisticated sound packages available, but there are also introductory ones which are generally quite straightforward. You can make a choice of particular types of sound (in the same way that you would choose a particular colour in a paint package) and then place a marker onto a simulation of a musical stave on the screen. The marker can be altered in length in order to make the note shorter or longer. Basically, you simulate putting notes on a stave and when you have completed the section, you can play back the music. A program of this nature allows for considerable experimentation until the student is happy with the overall effect. More sophisticated effects can be achieved by playing back a number of sounds from different musical instruments at the same time.

It is possible to link electronic keyboards to computers using a midi connection, and this will allow compositions played on the keyboard to be recorded on a computer, then manipulated electronically, perhaps by cutting and pasting sections, and then playing it back through the keyboard from the computer. Software also exists that prints out music after you have played in the notes through a keyboard.

Many computers come with simple sound software already installed, allowing you to record your voice or music and then to play it back after effects have been added.

## Sensing and measurement

One question that is often asked when discussing sensing software is why do we use a £1000 computer to measure temperature when we could use a £2 thermometer? And in many ways this is a very important question. Children should not get the idea that a computer should be used to do everything. They should be encouraged to think about the appropriateness of the equipment that they are using. But where a computer can be used to great effect is when the data can be collected over a much longer period than would otherwise be reasonable, i.e. overnight, or where lots of readings can be taken in a very short time, where the information can be very quickly and effectively displayed, and where that data can be analysed and compared.

Young children are therefore in a position to analyse graphical representation of data that they have collected, even though they would be unable to produce the graphs themselves. The computer is allowing us to change the teaching strategy – the analysis of graphical data, followed by the technical production of graphs by hand, with a clearer understanding of why graphs are useful.

The simplest of experiments can easily be used to help children relate a series of measurements to a graphical representation of that data. A temperature sensor could be left outside the classroom window and the computer set to record the temperature every ten minutes for a twenty four hour period. The graph, which can be instantly produced, can be used to discuss changes of temperature during the day, the differences between day and night temperatures, and how the graph for a day in December might be different from one for a day in July.

## Control

Most children's first experience of control will be when they use a floor robot. This can be made to travel forwards and backwards and to turn left and right by being given simple instructions such as *Forward 10* or *Turn Right*. Once children are familiar with the idea that they can control a vehicle by using simple instructions, they need to link the instructions together in sequences. For example, *Forward 10; Turn Right; Forward 10; Turn Right; Forward 10; Turn Right; Forward 10; Turn Right;* will produce a square with each side being 10 units long.

By now it is possible to develop this approach using a screen based robot or turtle. The turtle draws the shapes on the screen as it moves following the particular commands given. The next stage in programming, which is what this activity actually is, would be to identify instructions that could be grouped together in what is called a *procedure*. In this simple example the procedure might be called *Side* and would be made up of *Forward 10; Turn Right*. To draw a square now only requires a command such as *Side 4* which repeats the *Side* procedure four times.

Programs of this type do not only draw shapes but can also be used to control a number of switches. The switches can be on or off, and they can be controlled for very precise periods of time. The switches are attached to an interface which changes the messages from the computer, in the form of very small electrical signals, into much larger amounts of electric current which can be used to control lamps, buzzers and motors.

A further sophistication is in the way that the computer can also react to signals from the environment. We can use the ubiquitous example of the traffic lights to show what teaching and learning can take place through the concept of control. A simple circuit and a red, amber and green lamp can easily be operated by hand to simulate the pattern of traffic lights. But in a real life situation you need another set of traffic lights at right angles to the first set, and the pattern of these lights must be carefully co-ordinated with those of the first. It's getting a bit more difficult to physically organise this now, and remember that this pattern needs to take place 24 hours a day. This is obviously a role for a computer.

But we also know that, particularly at night when the traffic flow is much less, we need one set of lights to allow free flow of traffic on the main road until a vehicle needs to pass along the less busy road. This calls for a detector in the road that will know when a car is waiting to cross, and will cause the traffic lights to go through a complete cycle. So computers are very good at doing repetitive things. Children are introduced to the idea of control very much earlier in their school life when they use programmable vehicles. This uses exactly the same principle with the programmable vehicle switching motors on and off to make its way through a maze.

These ideas can be developed further by older students as they increase their understanding of control in design and technology, and mathematics.

## Framework programs

Imagine a central blank screen and a selection of pictures surrounding it. By clicking on a picture you can move it and place it anywhere on the screen, fixing it in place with a further click of the mouse. This is the concept behind framework programs which can be thought of as electronic 'fuzzy felt'.

A frequently used package is one that provides a map of the United Kingdom and a selection of weather symbols. Children can therefore easily make up their own weather map, without having to produce their own symbols, using a paint package.

Once you have a copy of the framework program, which has no content, you purchase individual add-ons which consist of a background and a selection of graphic images which you can place on the screen. The basic program also allows you to rotate and flip images and to change their size, although this last feature is fairly limited. A program of this type is incredibly flexible. Young children can use it to create their own illustrations of traditional stories, and older children can investigate mathematical concepts or be introduced to simple computer aided design. The program in effect is a limited drawing or paint program with integral clip-art, and as such provides an excellent introduction to using these types of packages. It is also a motivating way for young children to develop mouse skills.

Remember, however, that you can do nothing with the framework program itself – you need to buy the add-on packages of backgrounds and graphics.

## Content-based software

Looking through any computer software catalogue you will find an enormous and increasing range of titles covering all aspects of the school curriculum. Many will be databases covering subject specific material, and the best of these will be much more than a 'book on screen' incorporating meaningful interaction and appropriate multimedia elements, such as sound and video extracts. Much of the material will have been written initially for the home market, and will therefore incorporate entertainment elements such as quizzes and games. These so-called 'edutainment' products are often extremely well produced, and contain many useful activities which can greatly enhance the teaching in your classroom. However, the useful activities are often part of a longer adventure the intention of which is to give children freedom to find out which activities appeal to them. It might be that the activity which you feel is appropriate and the one which most excites your students are not the same. You will need to consider carefully how you make use of such resources in a focused way.

While it is relatively easy to evaluate a written resource, by the very nature of multimedia software, which is written in a branching rather than linear way, it is difficult to identify all the strengths of a piece of software, together with its weaknesses, without spending a considerable time using it. There are a number of organisations such as Teachers Evaluating Educational Multimedia (TEEM) and BECTa which provide independent reviews of much of this type of software, and this is likely to save a lot of time, and give you ideas about further titles which you might consider.

An overriding consideration must be: in what ways will the teaching and learning of the children or students in your classroom be enhanced as a result of using any of this material? If you do not believe that there is any enhancement, then do not bother using ICT in that particular way.

# CHAPTER THREE

# ICT in National Curriculum Subjects

In this section, consideration is given to the particular elements of ICT which are appropriate to subject areas of the National Curriculum. It is important to consider that the National Curriculum in place from September 2000 has very clear ICT links in all subjects, and some elements of ICT use are statutory. This section looks at each subject and considers the unique role which ICT has in that area. However, it does not consider the generic uses which are outlined in Chapter 2 of this book. It is, for example, clear that the World Wide Web can be used in every subject as a source of valuable up-to-date information. Similarly, all subjects could usefully encourage children or students to use a word processor to develop their written work.

## Primary

In primary schools, children will need to be introduced to the software toolkit which is described in Chapter 2. There are, however, a few issues which are of particular importance to teachers in this phase of education. When using software which has many components it is difficult to keep children's focus on one particular element of a program – when there are many and much more exciting avenues to explore. This might particularly be the case if children find themselves using products at school with which they are familiar at home. They might know more about the program than the teacher herself!

It will be in the primary school that children first make use of the WWW, and so it is there that they should be taught about the basic search strategies they will need. Huge amounts of time can be wasted by aimlessly 'surfing the net' and, while this will undoubtedly take up a great deal of children's time if they have access at home, it should not be considered an appropriate strategy to improve teaching and learning in school. This can be best achieved by providing a clear focus for any activity. It is likely that children will develop search strategies initially by using CD-ROM products, which, while still being extensive, will provide some constraint on the number of articles which will be identified.

It is most important that any 'free' searching of the WWW is undertaken by the teacher and that material is selected carefully before it is made available to children. A number of strategies exist for this filtering of information. If the school uses an Internet Service Provider (ISP) with a focus on educational use, you will find that when using this, children only have access to sites which others have identified as having educational worth. Alternatively, you can select the resources from the whole of the WWW, but download them onto your own school network. Children will appear to be searching the web, but in effect will only have access to the material which you feel is appropriate.

*Numeracy*

Computer programs can create very dynamic displays, showing, for example, ways in which shapes can be split up into fractions. It is true that this could be done physically in front of children, but the computer program does mean that many different examples can be demonstrated very quickly, and the labels of $\frac{1}{2}$ or $\frac{1}{4}$, for example, can clearly be linked on the screen. A program can visually display a simulation of the throwing of a dice, which the whole class can see on a screen. This allows more time to be spent on looking at more detailed aspects of probability, rather than spending the time throwing dice. However, in a situation like this, there needs to be a clear link between actually throwing a dice and the computer simulation. Without this, children will fail to see a link between how the random numbers were produced, thinking that the computer just 'made up some numbers'.

Database and graphing software allows young children to investigate situations that without ICT would be totally out of their reach. Children can link the number of boys and girls in a class to a representation of those figures in a bar or pie chart. They are able to say that this bar is longer, or this part of the pie is a bigger slice, because it represents the boys and there are more boys in the class than girls. They could also link temperatures taken on a manual thermometer outside the classroom at different times of the day to the different heights of bars on a bar chart. It was hottest in the middle of the day, so the bar is tallest in the middle of the day. This sort of work can be undertaken by children who would be incapable of actually drawing the bar or pie charts, but are capable of some evaluation of what the graphical representation shows. Here ICT is being used to do things that would have been impossible using more traditional teaching techniques.

The ease with which software can produce these results is, however, also a weakness, as it is quite possible to produce a pie chart showing the temperatures measured over a period of a week which means nothing! But an important teaching point can be made here. Just because a computer can produce a graph does not mean that it shows anything in a meaningful way. Similarly, a scattergram of two variables in a database can easily be produced, but are children able to analyse what it actually means? People still need a clear understanding of what they are trying to show, even though a computer can take away much of the time-consuming repetitive work.

Children can obviously make use of calculators when it is appropriate for them to do so. The use of calculators clearly will not replace their ability to undertake mathematical computation manually, but it does provide an opportunity to work with numbers which they have collected themselves. It also gives opportunities to explore number patterns, looking at what happens, for example, when you repeatedly add a number to itself. They need to be able to understand when use of a calculator is appropriate, and also to undertake a rough mental calculation, so that they are aware of when the answer they obtain on the calculator is approximately correct.

When children make use of a floor or screen-based turtle they receive immediate feedback in that it will travel along or draw a particular path. If this was not the route they expected they can instantly give a different instruction, and again see what happens. This interactivity provides a very real link between the instructions they write and the movements that are made. It is also very easy to start again. There are, however, times when this trial and error approach may not be the most effective style of learning, and children should be encouraged to have initial plans and strategies so that an activity of this kind becomes more than a game.

There are times when ICT can be used for particular teaching points but sometimes it might be excessively time-consuming to do so, and therefore inappropriate. A couple of children using a programmable toy to move backwards and forwards along a number line can easily be replaced by each individual child doing the same thing with others watching and contributing. Just because it can be done with ICT does not mean that it should be.

Spreadsheets can be used to investigate interlinked calculations. These types of activity always need to be undertaken when the children have a clear understanding of the basic calculations involved in the spreadsheet. Without this, no real learning is likely to take place. A spreadsheet which can show the profit and losses for a 'Bring-and-buy' sale, depending on increasing or decreasing the costs by different percentages, can only be useful if done when children are secure in their understanding of the ideas behind profit, loss and percentages.

## Literacy

Talking books and talking word processors give children immediate feedback and link the written word directly with the spoken word. Technically, the types of sound you obtain from these products are likely to differ. Talking books have a finite number of specific words and sentences which are read out while the program is running. This means that they can actually be a real person speaking the words, with each section being recorded as a separate sound file, being stored on the CD-ROM and played back when appropriate. It is just like a tape recorder. Increasingly, the products that are available include clear UK voices, whereas previously, many would have had American voices (and spelling in some cases!) The sound coming from most talking word processors is a digitised version of the words that are typed in. This is because there are an infinite number of words that could be typed into a word processor, so they cannot all be linked to specific sound files. This means that in some cases the speaking is not particularly clear, although the technology for both sound recognition and sound synthesis is developing rapidly and improvement will undoubtedly happen quickly.

Software which allows hidden or reordered text to be uncovered allows children the opportunity to explore the structures and patterns in sentences by making guesses or predictions. There are going to be times when, because of the learning objectives, it is inappropriate to use certain software. Handwriting will not be improved if the work is developed on a word processor. Spelling will not be improved if the AutoCorrect feature of many wordprocessors is functioning. Both teacher and children need to be clear about the advantages of using ICT in any particular circumstance.

Using word processing or presentation software as part of the literacy hour with the help of a large monitor that all the children can easily see is an extremely effective way of modelling the reading or writing process, and encouraging interactive participation by children at word, sentence or whole text level. It is possible to make effective use of animation effects that presentation software often has, in order to bring in particular endings, and include interesting illustrations. It is also possible to include children's own work as part of these presentations (by scanning in their artwork) which provides a personalised and motivating element to their work. Producing this type of resource is inevitably time-consuming, but if a group of teachers were happy to produce material for particular lessons and then share it with their colleagues, a useful resource could quickly be built up.

Increasingly, children will be undertaking much of their work on their computers at home. While you will want to encourage this, you need to be aware of compatibility and software virus issues, and fit in with the school policy on the subject.

Further details of ICT activities linked to other National Curriculum subjects can be found in *Information and Communications Technology in Primary Schools: Children or Computers in Control?* (Ager 1998).

## English

In the English National Curriculum there is a statutory requirement to use ICT-based sources and to make use of ICT to assist in the writing process

Some of the software tools can be used to enhance the teaching of English. A computer thesaurus, spellchecker and grammar checker can have many beneficial effects, but care needs to be taken to ensure that the automatic nature of many of these features does not remove the interaction between the student and the text. A spellchecker identifies misspelled words but not misused, correctly spelled words. A spellchecker does not really remove the requirement to read carefully through a piece of work when it is finished! A grammar checker often provides alternatives, and in some cases, misunderstands the sense of the sentence and so provides information that is not particularly useful. Some students might find the 'help' given to be rather confusing. A thesaurus can provide a list of alternative words which students can then select. They do, however, need to be aware of the nuances of the alternatives, as a straightforward replacement is often not appropriate. It is clearly also an important assessment issue to realise, when evaluating a piece of work, whether use has been made of such tools.

We have already discussed the ways in which text can be edited with the result that students can easily draft and re-draft their work. The facilities can also be used, for example, to change a piece of narrative text written in the first person into a piece written in the third person, meaning that only certain focused elements of the work would need to be changed. This would particularly emphasise the features of the two different forms of writing. A study of the significance of line length, and the effect of changing where the line break takes place in a piece of poetry can be explored very easily using this type of software. Teachers, however, can use the facilities of a word processor to edit text for a number of creative purposes. Increasing font size to assist visually impaired students, reducing sentence length for poor readers, replacing familiar words with synonyms to extend students' vocabulary and highlighting key words to support reading are some of the techniques which can be employed.

Students' writing can easily be made available to others using the school network or e-mail, so that collaboration between writers can be encouraged. The provisional nature of word-processed material means that it is easy to change any text, and the tracking options of many word processors allow for changes to be marked, so it is clear which participant has made which changes. This can, however, look a little complicated and it may be a function which is used only when there are a couple of collaborators.

Care must be taken when using a word processor in English to ensure that appropriate subject learning objectives are achieved. Just because the software has the ability to produce a wide range of different fonts and borders does not mean students should be encouraged to use them when they are inappropriate for the particular lesson outcomes.

Much of students' work in English relates to writing for a particular audience, and ICT can provide tools for doing this in a variety of ways. Using a video camera to record a class discussion, for example, can give you the opportunity to carefully observe each student's contribution, particularly focusing on their own role in the discussion rather than other people's. There will be times when it is useful to display text for all students to see, and to highlight particular features or to change its structure on screen to that students can contribute to the editing process. This will require either a large monitor, an LCD projector or an interactive whiteboard.

The World Wide Web (WWW) will give you and your students access to many different texts, but because of the ease with which material can be included, some of it may have undesirable elements, or just be an example of poor writing. It is important that you make yourself aware of any of the texts which students are freely accessing for use in their English work. In many cases, particularly when dealing with younger children, it might be more appropriate for the selection to be made for them. The teaching of reading strategies, particularly those related to selecting relevant or irrelevant information, or identifying bias in pieces of writing, takes on an increased importance when students are making use of material from the WWW. Different search engines and different search strategies will provide widely differing results. For example, some search engines give you an opportunity to focus on UK sites rather than those throughout the whole world. Students will need to know the importance of effective searching.

Writing for different audiences in different styles may allow the use of other pieces of software such as desktop publishing for brochures and leaflets or multimedia authoring software for computer-based information packages. This may involve the introduction or development of particular ICT skills within English teaching, and this should clearly be taken into account in planning. There are also opportunities to introduce students to appropriate ways of structuring material. They will be familiar with headings and sub-headings from print-based material, but they need to be aware of the use of icons and menus in many computer-based non-fiction textual information. The use of hot-links or hyper-links, unique to ICT systems, which immediately transfer readers to different parts of a document, or different documents and web-sites, needs to be discussed. Students using them will realise how such devices can convert a linear document into one with a branching structure. They can also be taught how to use them in their own work.

English teaching is an area in which the use of Independent Learning Systems (ILS) is quite well developed. An ILS is made up of the content, a system for recording individual responses and a management system. A very comprehensive account of the use of ILSs and their evaluation is to be found in *Integrated Learning Systems: Potential into Practice* (Underwood and Brown 1997). When looking at the progress which children made when working with the English language content Underwood and Brown observed that effectiveness seemed to depend to a great extent on the quality of teacher intervention. ILSs should not be seen as a teacher replacement but as an additional resource which can have beneficial results on children's literary levels. Indeed, in the USA where these systems were initially developed they do not appear to be eradicating literacy problems, in part perhaps because they are viewed as 'the' way in which English is taught.

Training teachers in the effective use of an ILS is seen as paramount if the best results are to be achieved. The feedback which it provides for teachers is extremely detailed and can produce a great deal of useful diagnostic information, but teachers need to know how to analyse the information in order to make best use of it. Interestingly, there was also some evidence that if the system was used by pairs of children in a cooperative way, performance gains were actually enhanced. It would seem that 'scaffolding' provided by both a colleague and a machine is better than than that provided by a machine alone.

The use of templates or writing frames particularly in word processing or web page design allows the teacher to provide structure for a piece of work. Because these are created electronically, they can easily be edited so they can be produced in a range of versions, some for those who need considerable support and others for those who require very little. This enables a differentiation in the activity to be provided quite quickly. In the case of more complex activities, such as the production of web pages, the use of a template can allow students to concentrate on the content of their writing rather than on the technical issues of producing a web page.

## Mathematics

In the National Curriculum for mathematics there are many examples of ways in which ICT can be used to produce graphs and diagrams, to make use of spreadsheets, databases, geometry or graphical packages and calculators and to make use of data obtained from ICT-based sources, as well as the statutory requirement that students should be able to produce shapes and paths by using ICT.

Dynamic geometry software allows students to move three-dimensional objects around on the screen, giving them the opportunity to look at them from many different points of view. With simple shapes such as cubes, the concrete representation is easily available in the classroom, so students are able to look at these shapes in reality. As shapes become more complex, the actual models are unlikely to be readily available, so the virtual model that dynamic geometry software is able to produce offers students something that without a computer they would otherwise not have had. It also allows students to experiment and hypothesise by, for example, increasing the number of sides for a particular shape, and seeing the effect that this has.

The WWW has a wealth of information which can be used for mathematical investigations. Even something such as investigating the lengths of routes between towns and cities can be done in a real-world situation using one of the many sites which provides such information.

Software is available which will allow mathematical symbols to be incorporated into word-processing documents. This is not a simple task and a judgement will need to be made if time should be spent putting together mathematical formulae on a computer screen, as opposed to using a pen and paper. In many circumstances it might be considered that a traditional approach would be more appropriate.

Because of the readiness with which the axes on a graph can be altered, it can be easy to explore the effects that changes can have on the overall impression which a graph gives. Starting the graph at a point other than the origin can, for example, imply much greater changes than actually exist, as can the selection of a very large scale for a very small area of a graph, which can imply great increases in profits, for example, until the actual figures are looked at more carefully.

Spreadsheets, graph-plotters and graphic calculators give students an opportunity to very rapidly obtain graphical representations of formulae, and also to investigate changes that can occur. Spreadsheets are going to have many uses within mathematics. If you prepare spreadsheets including hidden formulae, then students are able to input a range of values to try and discover what the formulae are. This causes students to interact quite extensively with the data, giving them opportunities to explore relationships. As students use calculators and computer software they also need to be taught to consider checking strategies, to ensure that they do not 'blindly' rely on the results they obtain. This has been important for some time when teaching students how to use calculators effectively (encouraging students to undertake a rough mental calculation to ensure an appropriate number of decimal places), and it is just as important when using more sophisticated software applications.

If we look at a fairly common mathematical activity we can consider how the use of ICT can enhance teaching and learning. Rolling a dice is the normal way to produce a set of random numbers, which can then be analysed. A spreadsheet can, however, produce random numbers very easily, and hence the list of random numbers can be readily and quickly produced, giving students more time to spend on working on the data. Hence the computer is relieving students of time consuming low level activities – shaking a dice and writing down the results – giving them more time to concentrate on analysing the random number data. However, care must be taken to ensure that students still realise the nature of random numbers in a concrete way. There are clearly dangers in getting a spreadsheet to generate a series of numbers 'as if by magic' in that the students may not be fully aware of what they actually mean. Relying solely on ICT is often not a good idea.

In mathematics it might be appropriate to use a whole range of cheaper, more portable hardware for particular activities. This will bring with it particular classroom management issues. Increasingly, students will wish to download the information on their portable devices to more powerful desktop machines and so you will need to know the most effective way of doing this. Increasingly, devices will have infra-red links which will make this an easy task, doing away with the need for extra leads and interfaces. However, you as a mathematics teacher will need to familiarise yourself with the technology required to do this.

Some of the software associated with mathematics is used solely in the subject and therefore you will need to ensure that part of your teaching will concentrate on the ICT skills that your students need to develop in order to use the software effectively. Most software is structured around a series of menus, many of which are common from program to program, so the basic structure of the software will be familiar to students, but they will need to be taught about the basic functionality of the program. In other cases, such as in your students' use of spreadsheets, you should be confident that students are competent in using the basic techniques of the software, and that they will only need to be given specific support in one or two more advanced elements.

Using software enables students to make changes very rapidly as they occur to them, and to try things out. While this is advantageous in many respects, it means that there is not necessarily a record of the students' progress throughout their experimentation. For students undertaking this kind of work in a more traditional environment, there will be pages and pages of (in some cases incorrect) calculations which provide the teacher with some evidence of what has been their thinking process. It is therefore clearly important that students are encouraged to keep some record of the steps they take, either electronically, by saving work at different stages in the process, or by taking notes by hand.

Programming languages are going to be used almost exclusively in mathematics lessons, and so a clear understanding of Logo or something similar is necessary to mathematics teachers.

For some considerable time there have been the coordination issues associated with mathematics and other subject areas such as geography and science. In best practice situations there is a clear strategy for ensuring that, for example, time/distance graphs in science are dealt with in a similar manner to the way they are introduced in mathematics, and at a time when the science work is building upon their existing mathematical knowledge. Using ICT in these situations does little to alter the coordination issue, but it might be that the overall ICT planning strategy across the curriculum might provide a more concrete issue to assist in the planning process.

Independent learning systems (ILS) are used as an important element of mathematics teaching in some schools. An ILS is made up of the content, a system for recording individual responses and a management system. Students work in front of the machines alone, with headphones on. It is a very solitary activity.

The power of the multimedia computers means that the information provided to children on screen can be exciting, motivating and educational. Some information is given, some question is asked, the student responds and then is given some feedback based on that response. The ILS systems, however, also manage the learning that goes on. If a student, for example, goes through a series of mathematical questions, getting them all right, the management system can automatically take the child on to the next mathematical ideas, occasionally slipping in a 'revision' question to make sure they have still remembered the ideas. One element of boredom is immediately relieved – children do not have to complete all 20 questions in an exercise when they understood the concept competently after completing three.

The National Council for Educational Technology (NCET) was commissioned by the then Department for Education to evaluate Integrated Learning Systems (ILS) and to explore their effectiveness in the UK education system. A very comprehensive account of the projects and their evaluation is to be found in *Integrated Learning Systems: Potential into Practice* (Underwood and Brown 1997).

It is worth highlighting one or two of the main findings of the evaluation. Students working with mathematical content in the earliest stages of the projects maintained their initial learning gains and this was evident both in groups that were continuing to use ILS and in those that no longer used such systems.

It is apparent that teachers need to be fully trained in the use of an ILS in order that children may achieve the greatest learning gains. As they became proficient and confident in its use they began to use the significant amounts of feedback on individual children's performance to inform future practice.

> This led to a small-scale classroom trial of basic number skills, which indicates that the children using ILS have gained an automaticity of skill not achieved by their classroom peers. There are also indications of a shift in attitude as these children were willing to take more risks and tackle unfamiliar material. (Underwood and Brown 1997)

However, ILSs should not be seen as a teacher replacement but as an additional resource which can have beneficial results on children's numeracy levels. Indeed, in the US, where these systems were initially developed, they do not appear to be eradicating numeracy problems, in part perhaps because they are viewed as the only fashionable way to teach mathematics. Training teachers in the effective use of an ILS is seen as paramount if the best results are to be achieved. The feedback which it provides for teachers is extremely detailed and can produce a great deal of useful diagnostic information, but teachers need to know how to analyse the information in order to make best use of it.

## Science

The National Curriculum statutory requirement for science is to make use of ICT sources, to represent and communicate qualitative and quantitative data using ICT and to use ICT for data logging.

It is relatively straightforward to create a neat table in a word processor, and for experimental findings to be input directly as they are taken. You do, however, need the computer there, with all the other experimental apparatus, and what sort of record will the students be able to keep? You might well decide that the results should be recorded by hand into the student's notebook, as you believe that the disadvantages of using the computer for this task far outweigh any advantages. Basically, the data will be collected in a neat table, but there is little else to be gained.

However, if the data is input into a spreadsheet, there are many more advantages to be accrued. Most fundamentally, the data can very quickly be displayed in a graphical form, and valuable learning time can be devoted to analysing what the graphs represent rather than merely producing them. It is in circumstances like this that the power of the computer allows you to do something in a different way and this enhances the learning experience of the students.

Spreadsheets also allow for the preparation of templates which students can use, but the opportunity also exists for templates with different amounts of structure to be made available, so that students with different levels of understanding can be directed to the spreadsheet which provides the most appropriate level of support. When students start to hypothesise about a particular scientific situation, ICT can quickly assist them by allowing them to try out their idea, and immediately seeing its effect. This is particularly true of children using a spreadsheet to assist in modelling.

ICT will allow students to explore phenomena that may occur too quickly or too slowly in reality. It also allows investigation of phenomena that would be too dangerous or prohibitively expensive to explore in the school situation. These are occasions on which you could consider using simulations or modelling to make the scientific understanding more accessible to the learners.

Simulations are probably the most powerful way in which computers can be used in science teaching because they provide new ways of teaching and learning that can only be undertaken by using ICT. A student using a simulation can rapidly try out things which would be impossible or impracticable done in any other way. Similarly, the rapid link between data and graphical representation can encourage students to further investigate the data collection as a result of a possible erroneous result shown up on a graph. Care, however, must be taken to ensure that students are really in a position to evaluate what a graph actually tells us. Just because a graph can be drawn does not mean that it is meaningful. Simulations such as Crocodile Clips give alternative approaches to more traditional practical activities, although care needs to be taken to ensure that they supplement rather than replace students' experiences of working with electronic components.

A great deal of resource material can be obtained from the WWW, but where you get the information from will depend a great deal on its source. Doing some research on smoking will get very different results depending on whether you use an anti- or pro-smoking Internet site. And how do you know if the information is accurate or whether it is coming from an accredited source? Both teachers and students need to be very aware of these issues of authenticity, accuracy and potential bias.

You also need to be aware of the implications of how you use ICT. Checking an American web site at 8 a.m. on your machine at home and finding it working well does not mean that it will download information effectively at 3 p.m. on the school network. Choosing a highly interactive web site may cause problems if your school computers do not have sufficient memory to download the images.

Demonstrations of experiments can be made far more effective if the results can be recorded automatically and displayed for the whole class to see. The results can then be transformed into graphs and a class discussion carried out to assist in analysing them. Issues such as safety need to be carefully considered, particularly when electrical equipment and cables are near heat and chemicals, such as in a cooling curve experiment. There may also be times when you want to compare manual and automatic data collection methods. This might be done by all groups repeating the experiment twice, or by half the class using one technique and the other half a different one. This is the only way in which you can identify the advantages and disadvantages of using ICT for such a purpose.

Students need to be very thoughtful in their use of ICT, and therefore, so do teachers. Students need to know very clearly when it might be appropriate to collect temperatures using a traditional thermometer, and when it might be better to use a temperature sensor. They also need to be informed that they are going to be assessed on their scientific knowledge and understanding, and not on how well the piece of work is presented. This means that you need to have a clear view on the ability of the student to understand, for example, the relationship between current and voltage, as opposed to his ability to display results using a graphing package. Requiring students to keep records of the progress of their work, together with selected printouts of work during development, may be a useful strategy to ascertain their progress.

As a teacher you might wish to make use of computer presentation software in order to improve the quality of a particular explanation. Inevitably, it will take some time to produce a high quality presentation, but it will be something which you or your colleagues could use over and over again. But there must be a reason for doing so. Your students are not going to be motivated by screen after screen of text but they might benefit from carefully produced, even simple, animations that will help explain a particular scientific concept. Incorporating multimedia elements from other sources might be useful. The use of animation is especially useful in helping students to understand particular topics.

Most museum web sites give up-to-date information about museum times, charges and special events. They can be used by teachers as a useful tool in planning a museum visit. The WWW gives teachers and students unlimited access to museum collections both before and after a visit.

## Design and Technology

The statutory requirement for design and technology in the National Curriculum is to make use of ICT-based sources, to use ICT equipment such as drawing or CAD software in order to design systems, and to simulate production and assembly lines including the use of ICT and control programs.

Because of the large elements of ICT which are introduced through this subject, it is inevitable that much ICT skill training will need to be undertaken within design and technology lesson time. Reduce this time to a minimum by building upon the ICT skills that students will have from work in other areas of the curriculum, and always emphasise the similarities between packages (Save, Print, Copy, Paste, Cut), before highlighting the significant differences. The advantage of most software being of a similar structure can reduce learning time considerably. Clearly, it is important that appropriate technical terminology is used, focusing upon it where they will not have come across it in other subjects (procedures, nesting, sequencing, etc.).

There might also be times when some of the more advanced features of programs may need to be introduced by giving students access to options menus. This may cause problems if students change options on programs and machines which other students will make frequent use of. When these students use the program and find out it is not functioning as they might expect, this will cause more work for the school's technical support team. Approaches to get over these problems may be to have machines designated for design and technology use, or to invest in network software which will allow settings of software to be matched to individual user names – whenever a certain user opens a program on the network, it has the setting that the user last used.

There is an increasing range of products for design and technology teaching, available either on the WWW or on CD-ROM. Many provide animations of the whole range of mechanisms which need to be understood. Care must be taken to ensure that an understanding of how something may function on screen is not divorced from an understanding of the physical artefact. Simulation software allows students to put together electronic circuits, as well as structural, mechanical and pneumatic systems on screen, and if they are connected correctly they will also work! In terms of electronic circuitry, this can save a large amount of time, as well as being much cheaper. You can experiment with different values of a component, for example, and if you select too high a voltage source, all the LEDs in the circuit will fail. But it is a very easy matter to replace them from the never ending supply available within the program.

However, there are two issues that need to be considered. If this type of software is used to the exclusion of real electronic components, then the students may fail to understand the nature of the simulation. The simulation becomes the real thing. When a focus of design and technology is clearly the design and manufacture of products, they really need to have appropriate experience with the real components. They will otherwise not be aware, for example, of the importance of ensuring that components are not overheated during soldering, or that the axles of gear wheels need to be very accurately parallel to each other if they are to function correctly.

Secondly, there is a danger that inappropriate strategies will be used in designing systems on screen. Because it is so easy to join components together, this 'trial and error' approach may be the favoured one unless students are encouraged to take a more systematic approach to their design. It is possible for students to design a system that clearly works, just by connecting more and more components together, but they will not have learned anything as a result of the activity.

Using the automatic features of some programs can expedite some mundane aspects of an activity and allow students to spend more time on the creative elements. The use of a 'Wizard' to produce a card layout, with all the printing automatically orientated in the correct direction for folding, or a brochure, which automatically prints out pages with appropriate pagination for producing an 8 or 12 page booklet of folded A4 paper, can ensure that more time can be spent designing the card or producing appropriate content for the booklet. There might, however, be times when you would want students to physically relate to the folds that need to be made, before making use of a computer package.

When students are more heavily involved in their own individual project work, it is important to be aware of their use of automated functions of software. This is not to say that you would not expect students to make effective use of software to make some tasks easier, but, for assessment purposes, you need to know which processes have been automated, and which have been undertaken by the student from scratch.

Using the WWW to access sites related to design, or some technical features related to health and safety, British standards or patents, for example, enables student to obtain material very quickly. Clearly, some of it may be too complex for the students involved, and this is where the importance of teacher intervention must be stressed.

Students will need to be able to make use of spreadsheets to model production costs, or nutritional content of a newly devised food product, for example. They can also be introduced to project planning software, which they can make use of when undertaking their own product development work. In the case of their use of graphics packages, it is likely that the features that they will wish to make use of for design and technology will be ones with which they are generally unfamiliar from their previous generic work. They will need to make use of Draw packages, rather than Paint packages, and the features of viewing 3-D designs from different angles, and adding different textures, shadows and colour to the finished product might well mean that they will need to be introduced to a new draw package, rather than extending their knowledge of an existing one.

It is also important to remember that the initial ideas are almost always most effectively undertaken with a pencil and paper, because it is quick and encourages additions and annotations. At no stage should it be expected that these sketches are re-done using a computer package. If the student does feel that they should be included as part of a high quality portfolio, which requires these sketches to be transformed electronically, then they should be electronically scanned into the document. It must also be remembered that the main purpose of any portfolio is to help students to develop their ideas. The use of ICT in presentation terms should not overshadow this purpose.

Similarly, teachers must realise that even though a student produces a high quality drawing which makes use of the full range of the computer's facilities, the actual design thinking may not be at a particularly high level. This has implications for the teacher, who must not be misled by the presentation, and for the student, who might lose motivation if negative comments are made about the design itself when they can see other students with poorer quality finished products being praised.

When using a CAD package, if a student's work is saved regularly under different file names it is possible for both the student and the teachers to see the development that has taken place as the design has evolved. This is a great advantage over a traditionally drawn design, where, to get similar information, regular photocopies would need to be taken. Technically, it is important that students save their work under sensible and different file names, so that it is possible to open them all up to identify the development. If this is going to be an important element of teacher assessment, it is clearly also important that adequate back-up files of students' work are maintained. If files are automatically saved, they will automatically overwrite the earlier version.

Computer aided manufacture (CAM) is an area which many schools are developing. It usually makes use of very specific pieces of hardware and software, which are often also connected to a computer. Most commonly, products can be designed using a computer aided design (CAD) package and, with the computer connected to a computer controlled milling machine or lathe, the product can then be automatically manufactured. Similar approaches can be undertaken with computer controlled sewing or knitting machines and vinyl cutters, for example. Again, consideration needs to be given to the learning outcomes of such an activity. A computer-based sewing machine can produce intricate embroidery designs, which are stored on floppy discs, in a very short time. Alternatively, there are ways in which a student's own design can be scanned into the machine, and subsequently that design is automatically embroidered. This requires some detailed technical knowledge to identify which aspects of the student's design should be embroidered in which colour.

In the first case therefore, all a student is doing is automatically embroidering an existing design onto a garment. They are learning about the technical possibilities, but they are not involved in producing the design themselves. In the second case they are involved in the creation of the design, and in a more detailed understanding of the technical issues. However, in the production of one item with this design, was it appropriate to use this technology when the same time could probably have been spent learning how to use the machine to produce a one-off manual piece of embroidery? If the purpose of computer-aided manufacture is the production of multiple high quality products, when is it appropriate to use the technique to produce just one?

Although computer control obviously has a high profile in design and technology work, it too should only be used as appropriate. There are many electronic and mechanical products which will not benefit in any way from the addition of some computer control. Software of this kind does not always lead students to the most appropriate solution if it is the simplest. For example, there may be times when a simple switching circuit is what is required rather than the extensive electronic solution which can be designed using some software.

Students developing their skills in control technology will need to link ready prepared models, or ones they have built themselves, to computers via interfaces. There are also opportunities to investigate sensors which can be incorporated into control applications. A temperature sensor will detect overheating, for example, or a light sensor will ensure that a particular control function will only operate when it is dark. It is therefore important that appropriate hardware can be taken over to more general ICT facilities, or that appropriate ICT facilities, together with interfaces exist within the design and technology departments. The number of computers and interfaces which you have available will have considerable influence on the way in which this element of work may be taught. However, design and technology teachers are familiar with sharing out the use of limited and expensive facilities, so this area of workshop management will cause few problems. Health and safety issues, again very familiar to design and technology teachers, will also need to be considered, particularly relating to the positioning of computer equipment in workshops where hand and machine tools are used.

There are a large number of pieces of control software and it is likely that the design and technology department will have a major role in choosing the most appropriate product. Care needs to be taken to strike a balance between offering the range of facilities that may be required but which is also simple enough to be used by students who are new to the topic. It might be that you look for software which can be customised to provide limited facilities for novice users, or invest in two different products. It is important to avoid excessive confusion by using too complex a product when developing the ideas of control. It is again important to realise that many of these products have libraries of procedures which students may access. When students undertake a task, are you aware if they have worked out the problem for themselves, or merely copied the procedure from the library?

Design and technology teachers will inevitably need a high level of technical understanding of ICT as it links to the work they are undertaking on a regular basis. They will need to be familiar with sensing and control software and hardware, as well as a full range of peripherals including plotters and digital cameras, which offer many opportunities for students to keep a detailed record of the development of their projects.

There are many opportunities within design and technology to put the use of ICT in society into context. Many everyday artefacts are increasingly involving an ICT element, and the advantages and disadvantages of this can usefully be discussed in the context of the students' own designs.

## Geography

The statutory requirements for geography in the National Curriculum include being taught how to use ICT to help with geographical investigations such as using mapping software and spreadsheets, to make use of ICT-based sources and to use ICT to communicate their ideas.

Use of word processors for the more formal report writing, e-mail for informal communications with students both in this country and abroad, desktop publishing for the production of leaflets or brochures about particular topics and the use of spreadsheets to model particular geographical situations will ensure that students develop their more generic ICT skills within geography. Here we will look at applications which are more likely to occur only in geography.

Clearly, the vast developments which have been made in mapping software offer great opportunities for the geography classroom. Maps of most areas of the world are available from web sites, and may be freely printed out for individual student study. Mapping software, which allows students to plan routes from place to place within the United Kingdom is also available, giving them the ability to focus in on very small areas, or to zoom out to get a much bigger picture. Encyclopaedia products often offer high quality mapping facilities together with a wealth of up-to-date data about the particular city or country. Useful comparisons can be made between similar data from a number of sources, perhaps a CD-ROM product and then a WWW site. Issues such as which is likely to contain the most reliable information can then be addressed. You always need to consider whether the use of a traditional map or atlas might be more appropriate for some activities.

Use can also be made of students' capability to use other pieces of generic software. If students copy a basic map into a piece of presentation software or a graphics package, then they are easily able to annotate it using appropriate software tools. They can label parts of the map, include additional lines to emphasise boundaries, and even remove elements – this is what this location would look like if the new road scheme were to be approved, for example. Teachers and students can also make much of the animation effects which some programs offer in order to illustrate, in a clear way, the changing features of the area they are studying.

Because of the wealth of maps which are now available and easily downloadable for incorporation into a student's own piece of work, there are going to be very few times when students actually need to draw their own maps. As a professional, you need to determine if this is a skill which you feel students should develop, and therefore you must create opportunities for practising it; or is it an outdated activity whereas students' use of 'electronic' maps is totally appropriate? Inevitably, as technology advances, some traditional skills are no longer needed, but new ones are required to take their place. (Log tables and slide rules are now entirely replaced by calculators.)

More sophisticated pieces of mapping software allow for more detailed interaction with the maps. In particular, the ability to look at information in different 'layers' allows a complex map to be made much simpler by choosing to view only certain features, such as contour lines, initially, and then adding roads to see what patterns can be observed.

It is now possible for schools to purchase equipment which allows them to monitor the local weather over 24 hour periods. All the data can be stored on a computer and it can then be analysed as appropriate. It will allow your students to undertake a wide range of comparisons, for instance with the weather in the school last week, last month or last year, or comparisons with data from other places in the world, from a wide range of sources, e.g. newspapers, radio, TV, satellite or cable TV and the WWW. Care needs to be taken that the capital investment is well used. For example, weather data is readily available from the Internet for many locations in the world. If the data in your own school is collected automatically and remotely, without the students realising the methods and equipment which enable it to be collected, you may just as well make use of the computer data, without collecting your own. If, however, the students have an active role in siting, maintaining and in other ways interacting with the equipment which does the sensing, and if they are also clearly involved in the software which they use to interface between the equipment and the screen, then equipment of this kind can add a great deal to student learning in this area of the curriculum. An activity like this also allows you to discuss points such as data-logging equipment giving you the opportunity to take readings 24 hours a day, when manual methods would make this impracticable.

Geography gives you the chance to look at issues closely related to increasing use of ICT throughout society. It would be possible, for example, to predict what may happen to particular communities over a period of time, as more people are able to work from home using a computer connected to their work, using high speed cabling. The effects on housing, road developments and siting of offices are all highly pertinent to a discussion of this type.

Animations, many of which are available on CD-ROMs are often useful to help explain dynamic features. A professionally produced animation of plate movements might help the learning of many students compared with what you might previously have produced as a series of sketches on the whiteboard. This is not to deny that rough sketches in addition to the animation may be a very effective aid to teaching, and when you have access to an interactive whiteboard it will be possible to coordinate all these elements together. In your current planning you want to make the best use of the ICT facilities that you have at the moment, but also have a vision of what software and hardware you might need in the future to assist your teaching.

Geography departments have for many years been at the forefront of using computers to obtain satellite imagery, using satellite receiving equipment connected to a computer. Many students in the early 1990s will have been motivated to see 'real' images of the United Kingdom appearing on the computer screen, showing a picture of what the weather was actually looking like a few minutes earlier. They were looking at 'live' data. This is an area, however, where the WWW has rapidly superseded the need to purchase such specialised pieces of equipment, as there are plenty of web sites where this information is readily accessible without the need for considerable setting up time. In a rapidly developing area such as ICT it is always worth consulting with colleagues to ascertain what the best way forward may be. Being a couple of years behind the 'cutting edge' may in some cases allow you to learn valuable lessons which will save you both time and money. There are, however, clearly dangers in being too far behind in terms of ICT developments.

An important element of geography is fieldwork, and the use of notebook computers with appropriate software and additional hardware allows data to be easily collected in the field and then analysed in detail on return to base. To use equipment in this way requires students to be competent in connecting additional hardware, in operating the software and in downloading the information to appropriate storage devices. Initially, you may just be given the hardware, and have to make the most effective use of it that you can. In the future, you will need to know what specification is necessary for the type of work that you want to undertake, and something about the interfaces themselves.

Much of geography is about peoples and places, and illustrations offer opportunities to enliven and enrich students' work. Particularly in local geographical activities, photographs have always been useful but now digital cameras allow students to produce illustrations extremely quickly and relatively cheaply. These can then easily be incorporated into their work and annotated appropriately. As a teacher, you may have used a series of slides to introduce a particular topic. The ease with which good quality annotations can be added to a series of photographs using a presentation package may encourage you to consider altering your approach. A large TV can be used as a monitor, although an LCD projector will be the preferred method of display. Once the resource is prepared it can be easily distributed around the department for other staff to use, and if all members of the department are responsible for producing one presentation, this will, in the end, save a lot of time.

Different types of camera have different storage media, and different resolutions for storing images. The higher the resolution, the better quality the image will be. At one end of the spectrum a mega pixel camera (the images are made up of more than a million different sections) and a good quality photo printer, printing on shiny photographic paper, will provide you with a finished product equivalent to a normally processed 35mm photograph. The advantages you have with this approach are the immediacy and the facility to digitally alter the photographic image using graphics software. You can add features to or remove people from the photo, for example, or add permanent annotations if desired. As you purchase cheaper cameras, the picture resolution decreases, but these pictures are often good enough to incorporate into desktop published documents or onto web sites. Cameras now exist with which short video extracts can be recorded as well as stills, with a file size sufficiently small to allow the images to be transmitted over the Internet. The quality of these movie images is not particularly high, but it will again give students a degree of immediacy to their work.

As in other subjects, there may be times when you feel that the students' work could well be published on the school's web site. In geography, this would be particularly relevant if it involved geography topics related to the local community. As well as an increased motivational aspect for students, it will give them a real audience for which to produce their material, and it will also provide appropriate publicity for the geography department!

## History

The statutory requirements for history in the National Curriculum require students to make use of ICT-based sources, and to communicate making use of ICT.

Data files of historical events spreading over large periods of time can be used for analysis so that, for example, hypotheses about long-term trends can be devised and tested. Because there is now an enormous range of sources of information, it is possible for students to study the different emphases which different accounts may provide. This can lead them to look at records of events at the time and discussions of them written at a later date, and to learn how accounts of events today may vary depending on the stance of the authors.

It is obvious that text is not always the best way to describe causes and effects, and diagrammatic representations can easily be produced using appropriate software. In this particular example you need to be careful about the selection of the software. An appropriate selection will be one that allows students to move easily blocks of text, arrows and perhaps images around, so that the diagram can be developed on the page. Desktop publishing and presentation software would be the ideal choices for this activity. Many sophisticated word processors will allow you to produce the same finished product, but it will be a much more complex ICT activity as graphics cannot be positioned so easily in these types of packages. It is almost certain that your learning objectives for the lesson will be related to the history of the situation, rather than ICT skills, and so you must advise students to use the most appropriate software.

There is some simulation software available for history which might show how settlements develop over time, the courses of particular wars or the growth and decline of industries. In these, the student will be able either to simulate the decisions that were made and see the effect, or more creatively, explore what might have happened if different decisions had been made. Students should be aware that while simulations can offer insights into historical events, they are computer programs which have been written by a particular author, with a particular view of history. This provides students with an opportunity to evaluate these products' historical validity.

History offers a wealth of opportunities for students to present their ideas on historical issues to a wide range of audiences. Students can therefore be encouraged to make use of a wide variety of ICT including video productions, multimedia presentations or desktop publishing to produce, for example, newspapers or guidebooks. Inevitably, work involving this type of ICT will take longer to cover the historical content than might have been taken using more traditional teaching techniques. The advantages of such an approach can be the deeper level of learning which can be involved and the increased motivation which such activities engender. If you are working with students who are already technically capable of using ICT, then you have less of a problem, but if there is a need for you to develop ICT skills before your students engage in the historical activity, this cannot be done on an ad hoc basis, but needs to be built into the whole-school approach to cross-curricular ICT.

In Year 9, for example, the history department might agree to cover the technical aspects of multimedia productions, through a history project, which other subject areas can pick up on in Years 10 and 11. If the activity is part of some group work, the time problem could be alleviated by each group undertaking work in different themes, and then the other groups making use of the material to enable them to learn about each topic. At a simple level, each group could produce a presentation which they gave to the rest of the group. At a more sophisticated level, each group could produce a multimedia teaching pack incorporating information and questions, which every other group then had to work through. Those materials of particularly high quality could then be made available to students in subsequent years, ideally over the school Intranet.

Tabulating information obtained from text-rich sources is a useful tool to ensure students interact with material. Deciding on how the table may be produced is important to get the best out of the activity. There would seem to be at least five approaches. They make up their own table on paper, and fill it in by hand; they copy a table from the whiteboard and fill it in by hand; you provide a photocopied table which they fill in by hand; they make up their own table on a computer and fill it in on the keyboard; they use a template including a table which you have already prepared and fill it in at the keyboard. All of these methods could satisfy your subject learning outcomes. Some require whole-class access to a computer, others require no ICT at all. Some would take a lot longer than others.

The method you choose would obviously depend on various factors. Do you, for example want students to copy the words from the textual material and paste them straight into the table, ready for some limited editing? Do you believe that this is more appropriate than getting your students to copy out the appropriate material by hand? In schools where students are used to having ready access to computers the ICT options are probably the most appropriate. If you needed to book an ICT suite for this 20 minute activity, moving students backwards and forwards from room to room, then it would probably not be appropriate. You as the professional in your particular situation need to decide, but most importantly, in this rapidly developing field, you might decide that the appropriate approach this year may not be the best one next year.

Databases are of great use within history, allowing graphical representations of data to be quickly produced. Initially students will probably be provided with the field headings for databases which they produce, but as their skills develop they will need to understand that field headings have to be carefully thought about if they are going to be able to analyse information which they put into their databases. If you, for example, have a column in your database for 'Year' then inputting single years will enable sensible graphical representations to be produced. If, however, an event took place over several years, and you are required to enter '1939-1945', then the data will be in an inappropriate form and will not allow sensible graphs to be produced. Similarly, the nature of data input into a database needs to be carefully considered, so that useful analysis can be undertaken. Consider a local census database which a student wants to build up from paper-based records. One of the questions that you may want to ask is what is the most common occupation in the village. It might be that when looking at the data, it would be more useful to include generic descriptions of say shopkeeper or farmer, rather than grocer or shepherd, which would allow for the graphs to show a variation of different occupations. This might not be the case if you were to include individual job descriptions, which in a small database might lead to there just being one of every category.

Students will obviously want to make use of the World Wide Web and CD-ROMs to search for sources of information. You should be able to expect that they are aware of suitable searching strategies, but you might well wish to discuss with the class as a whole the question of which keywords would be particularly appropriate for the historical research undertaken.

When students are engaged in relatively long pieces of work, the fact that the information can be stored at different stages can allow you to see how their ideas and thoughts developed. This means that students must be aware that they are required to save their work in a series of different files, and that they should be given an appropriate naming structure. This is a different approach to the one that is normally taken, where 'Save' saves the current work and overwrites the previous version of the file. This means that you only have one piece of work, i.e. the one that contains the most recent changes. As a matter of course, students and teachers should make regular backups of their work to different storage devices (floppy disc, second hard disc drive, high capacity back-up drive or re-writable CD-ROM are possible choices).

## Music

The statutory requirement for music in the National Curriculum is to use ICT to capture, change and combine sounds.

In music, it is likely that many of your students will already be familiar with many of the possibilities which using ICT affords. Their enthusiasm obviously needs to be built upon and developed. It is therefore important that students are challenged to take on new projects and develop their expertise.

Many keyboards available now effectively have a computer inside them, allowing compositions to be stored in memory and then replayed. In the same way that the word processor allows text to be quickly restructured, computer software exists which allows the pitch and length of musical notes to be altered very easily, giving students the opportunity to experiment with the format of music.

Access to the WWW allows a wealth of information relating to a wide range of musicians and musical styles to be researched and investigated at first hand. Many web sites also allow for extracts of the composer's work to be downloaded. The WWW is likely to have a profound effect on the way in which recorded music is played and distributed. Good CD-quality sound is now the norm. CDs were designed specifically to distribute high quality digital sound. A typical piece of popular music would take up about 50 Megabytes of memory – a CD can hold about 600 Megabytes. There are now ways of compressing the digital information to such an extent that near CD-quality sound can be achieved using up typically 3 or 4 Megabytes. These are called MP3 files. There are an increasing number of web sites where pieces of music can be downloaded and stored, and then played on your computer. There are also portable MP3 players which are able to store musical data in memory, and which can then be used like a Walkman.

The effect of this is that it is possible to distribute music far more easily than through the traditional record company route. This means that you are able to explore the work of composers who have not obtained recording contracts, and that your students are able to put their work up onto the web for the whole world to listen to. As in most work related to the Internet, students need to be aware of the implications of this ever increasing access to material. They need to be taught to evaluate, perhaps more effectively than they might have done before. Students can download text files from the WWW, and with a little editing can pass it off as their own work. Students can also do this with music files, and teachers must be aware of these possibilities.

CD-ROMs exist which include a recording of a piece of music together with detailed analysis of the way in which the musical ideas have developed. Parts of the music are able to be selected and played very easily. This was possible with vinyl records (although it was difficult to find exactly the right position), easier with CDs, (where counter positions could be recorded) and extremely easy with CD-ROM software where this type of access can be built into the program. Here ICT is not doing something that was impossible before, but it is making something much easier, less time-consuming and therefore more likely to be actually carried out. There are also CD-ROMs which provide you with images and samples of the kind of sounds made by a wealth of musical instruments from around the world. No teacher or school would ever have had the resources or skills to show what the instruments look like or to hear what they sound like either by themselves or in combination with other instruments. In this mode of use we are doing something that previously would have been impossible.

Sophisticated keyboards offer yet a further tool which teachers and students can use to explore the differences between the sounds made by different instruments. Just using one piece of equipment the teacher can demonstrate an enormous range of different instruments. However, there are also opportunities to discuss the disadvantages of using this type of approach. Students must realise that there is still a desire for musicians to learn 'real' instruments, because although they can be reasonably replicated, there are elements of their sound and expression which cannot be emulated by an electronic version of the instrument.

When students use ICT to write compositions they are always able to save earlier versions of their work. This means that you, as the teacher, have clear evidence of the way in which the composition has progressed, and the students are able to return to an earlier version if they discover that a particular route they have taken is not satisfactory. Computer software is available which will print out proper musical notation, having input the details of some musical notes into a computer. However, there may be times when you want students to actually produce a hand-written score so that they are able to interact with the material more closely and with a better understanding.

The recent history of recorded music is linked firmly to ICT itself, so music is an ideal medium through which some technical elements of ICT can be taught. It is therefore important that the correct terminology is used when talking about its role in music, so that students are not confused when they deal with similar issues in other parts of the curriculum.

A computer with appropriate software can form the basis of a multi-track recording studio. This provides great creative opportunities, but their effective use is a far from trivial task. Students must be taught how to make the most of the facilities which they have and be given appropriate instruction, both in the technical elements of the work and in the ways in which effective results can be achieved. An interesting issue to consider here is whether the technology is the important issue or the finished product. Imagine a student who wanted to write a song in four-part harmony, and who wanted to perform it completely by themselves.

This could be achieved either with considerable technical support from a teacher or other students, with the finished recording matching the student's objectives, or the student could be given additional tuition as to how to use the equipment to achieve the desired result and then complete the whole task themselves. The two lessons would have two different learning outcomes, although the finished product might be identical. In one, the additional element was the greatly enhanced ICT capability which the student would have. It would, however, probably have taken much longer from start to finish of the process.

Like the Wizards or macros of word processors, ICT in music has standardised ways of doing particular tasks. Keyboards often have pre-set rhythms or automatic backing tracks associated with particular chords. While an automatic rhythm might be appropriate for one piece of music, it may not be appropriate for everything, so the teacher has a vital questioning role encouraging the students to reflect on the quality of the music produced, and how best to achieve high quality results, although not necessarily using the easiest or quickest technique. The support available with some software can achieve very formulaic and bland results.

## Art and design

The statutory requirement for art and design in the National Curriculum is that students should make use of ICT as one of the materials and processes which they encounter in their learning.

Using an art package gives many opportunities to experiment with the wide range of effects that are possible including: reversing colours, solarisation, posterisation, altering contrast or changing an image to a line drawing. Colours can be changed very quickly, and images and parts of images can be cut, copied and pasted into new positions.

Care needs to be taken to ensure that the sophisticated tools which some art packages contain are used sensibly and in moderation. In the same way that many people's first attempt at desktop publishing includes multiple fonts, a wide range of colours and a number of irrelevant pieces of clip-art, first attempts at using art packages can overuse some of the facilities available. Students need to understand the similarities between techniques used in more traditional media and those used in computer work, and be aware of the power of the techniques which are only possible using software. This is an important point because clearly students need to realise the advantages and disadvantages of a wide range of techniques. Collaborative working can be encouraged using this electronic medium, because of the ease with which students can say 'Lets try this' and 'What happens if we do that?' Regular saving of the image, under different names, can be used to provide you with evidence showing the way in which a piece of work developed.

There are going to be times when you want to use illustrative material as you talk about the work of different artists. This is appropriately done on a large display monitor or using an LCD projector. At other times you might be happy that a few students are working in electronic media on a few computers within the art and design area while other students are working with more traditional media. Then again, you might need to book a lesson in the computer room, so that all students can engage in creating work utilising art packages.

Most art packages are likely to be of a format familiar to students, consisting of menu bars and drop-down lists. However, although the structure may be familiar, the actual functionality of every item is likely to require some specific teaching. In Chapter 2 of this book there is a discussion relating to the use of paint or draw packages. However, there are many other features of art software, some of which can be relatively straightforward while others are extremely sophisticated and complex. There are going to be stages in your use of such software where you will need to teach students exactly how to use the facilities. There may be times when you can ask students to 'find out' what some of the features do, but it is almost certain to be more profitable if you focus upon particular aspects of the program and provide ICT skills tuition on how the technique can be used. As an art and design teacher you will be unable to expect that the sophisticated detail of art packages will have been covered previously, although you should be certain that all students are happy to load, save, print, cut, copy and paste and that they will know how to search for particular features.

You will need to understand the functioning of the more complex art packages quite well, as you will also need to be able to make adjustments to the program, such as limiting the range of colours or some of the other functionality of the program. You should not underestimate the amount of time it will take to really understand how a complex computer program can be used, and realistically, there may be a need for off-site or on-line ICT skills based training to supplement your existing skills. Students will also need to be taught the appropriate terminology linked to this area of work, and understand technical issues whenever they are appropriate for this kind of work. Consider, for example, the appropriate type of colour cartridge which needs to be in a colour printer for draft or for colour photo quality work, or the ways in which a large graphics image can be transferred from one machine to another.

It is clear that using a computer art package does not make it easier to produce an artistic piece of work. However, where freedom of media is given, some students may spend much longer practising the skills relevant to their use of graphics software, rather than developing other artistic skills such as freehand drawing. This clearly needs to be considered, particularly as it relates to assessment. Throughout their work in art, students will need to be questioned and challenged about their use of particular media. There must be opportunities to discuss the ways in which some work is undertaken far more appropriately by using more traditional media.

The automatic features of many video or digital cameras allows you to produce time lapse photographs. Use of art packages and the ability to save images at any stage in the process can lead to effective and relatively simple animations. Creating a complex picture using a piece of presentation software, and then duplicating this image many times, and then removing components from subsequent images can then lead you to build up an image from a blank screen up to the completed picture.

The WWW provides unparalleled access to images from art galleries throughout the world. This can supplement the supply of resources which you hold in other forms. It is also possible to develop a class art gallery on the school web site, which gives students a worldwide audience for their work.

Other hardware that you will need to consider when undertaking work with graphics are scanners, drawing pads and good quality colour printers. A scanner converts the physical image on a sheet of paper into an electronic image with each pixel being designated either a particular shade of grey for black and white photographic images, or a different colour for colour images. Once they are converted into a digital form, they can then be manipulated by computer packages, or just printed out using a printer. Digitising tablets or computer drawing pads consist of a pressure sensitive drawing board which is connected to a computer and can be used with a range of art packages. A pen-like stylus is used to draw on the board and the movements are replicated on the screen – there is no mark made on the board itself. The stylus can also operate like a mouse in selecting functions of the software.

The most common types of colour printers are ink-jet and laser printers. Ink-jets are currently the most reasonably priced, although the quality achieved from a laser printer is much higher. Colour ink-jet printers either use four individual colour cartridges – black, cyan, yellow and magenta or a single colour cartridge which contains reservoirs of blue, cyan and yellow ink. Although usually more expensive, the versions with the four cartridges usually give a better overall quality, because the black images are created from black ink, rather than a mixture of blue, cyan and yellow, which can give a generally brown colour. The cartridges also only need to be replaced when they are each completely empty, whereas with the combined cartridge, it has to be replaced as soon as the first of the colours runs out or you get some very funny coloured images!

Whatever type of graphics package you use, a lot of memory is required both for storing the image and for manipulating it. Often you will want to use a scanner to transfer children's artwork from more traditional media to a digital format for further manipulation. A normal floppy disc holds approximately 1.4 Megabytes of information. For images, particularly full colour ones which are scanned into the computer, this may not be enough. This means that scanning in the image, manipulating it and integrating it into other work, may need to be done on the same machine, because there is no way in which the image can be made portable. Alternative approaches are to ensure that the resolution and size of the image are reduced so that they only take up approximately 1.2 Megabytes of memory and therefore can be saved onto a completely empty floppy disc, to use the newer floppy disc drives which can hold much more information, or to link computers together, either on a full network, or through a temporary direct cable connection.

The machine which is going to manipulate the image not only needs a lot of hard disc storage but also a lot of random access memory (RAM), because the image has got to be held in memory while it is being worked on. Because of the high memory requirements, the computer program may well run extremely slowly, which can be frustrating to students, who end up frantically clicking in the mouse and consequently causing many unexpected effects to occur. In summary, if you use a computer for image manipulation it needs to be a high specification machine, with a fast processor, large amounts of memory and an extremely large hard disc. Without this you will still be able to use paint and draw programs, but the more sophisticated activities will be frustratingly slow or impossible.

## Modern Foreign Languages

The statutory requirement for modern foreign languages in the National Curriculum is for students to make use of ICT-based sources and to use ICT to improve their accuracy and presentation.

Word processors are likely to be used to allow students to work closely with text in ways which would be difficult without ICT. If given a piece of writing in the present tense they can focus on those elements which need to be changed in order to put it into the past tense without having to type the whole passage out, and they are therefore saving time. However, it is also important to be aware that if students continually engage in this type of activity they may not be gaining experience of writing their own original material. There clearly needs to be a balance, to ensure that all modern foreign language learning outcomes are covered in an appropriate period of time. While students will be familiar with the use of wordprocessors, it may be necessary to teach them the ICT skills involved in using accented characters. It will also be appropriate to teach them the technical ICT language they might require to speak about their use of ICT in their target language. (Although 'e-mail' would seem to be a fairly universal term!) As students are likely to be familiar with many of the features which are available in the software, it is important that they do not spend too much time making use of those which are not appropriate to the subject-based work. Although it might be appropriate to produce a chart from some data related to a foreign country, which they put into a database, the time taken by the technical task of producing the chart must be measured against the time during which they are interacting with the foreign language.

There are an increasing number of software packages which provide multimedia resources, allowing students, on an individual basis, to hear the language being spoken, as well as having features such as highlighting the words as they are spoken. In this situation, students will, of course, be wearing headphones. Most software of this nature currently does not have the facility to save the student's repeated responses, either for individual review or for assessment by the teacher, but with the increased sizes of computer discs and the increasing use of voice recognition software, this will soon be a reality. This will, in effect, mean that the coordination of video material and tape recorders for recording responses will be carried out within a computer. It is vital to realise that although a student is using a technique which would appear to be independent, effective learning will only take place if there is appropriate intervention by the teacher. Even when using sophisticated software which provides the students with automatic feedback, it is important to intervene to ensure that the students are understanding or making use of the feedback. A student who scores highly in a vocabulary recognition activity, for example, may not necessarily be able to use those words in appropriate contexts, so the subject learning outcomes must be clearly linked to the ICT-based activities with which the students are provided.

Other text manipulation programs allow text to be analysed and give opportunities for students to focus on particular elements of text and to look for patterns. This might involve a series of words which have their endings removed, which need to be replaced by the students, or more traditional cloze-type activities where words are deleted from sentences, and students are asked to predict what the missing words might be. In some cases, this type of software will not record students' responses automatically, and they will therefore be required to print them out for the teacher to comment upon. In other cases, responses could be recorded, and it is important that teachers have a good understanding of how the information can be retrieved so that it can be made use of in a formative way. It is also important that when the software is purchased, it is clear what features it has, as this will have very clear implications for the way in which it will be used.

Concordancing software allows for the automatic indexing of text, so that terms can easily be searched for. Most commonly, the software would be used on a book such as the Bible, so that individual words can easily be located in an enormous text. This would be very difficult to do any other way than using ICT. In most cases, you would access a web site where the material has already been processed, and you just input the words for which you wish to search. However, you can also use concordancing software to analyse text of your own choice.

Modern foreign language teachers have for a long time made use of audio-visual source material as an integral part of their teaching. The developments of new technology have just made some aspects of this much easier to manage. With the increased size of computer hard discs and the compression of computer files, video files can easily be run on a computer, and they can be selected very much more easily than finding the correct place on a video. Compare finding the start of a music track on a cassette tape and a CD. You can envisage a time when your own notebook computer will have all the video and sound elements which you might want to use in your teaching, and this could be regularly connected to the large display monitor, LCD projector or interactive whiteboard in your classroom. If the facility is permanently available it is more likely to be used regularly, even for quite short elements, where previously the time required to set up a video recorder may have deterred you from using it.

The communications aspect of ICT is of considerable importance in modern foreign languages where it provides opportunities to experience the language in a real context. Cable and satellite broadcasts allow students to study television in the appropriate countries. Students can also access web sites which are written in foreign languages. There are even web sites which enable you to translate the content of sites into other languages, and these could be studied to see how accurate they were in the translation process. Students can also be guided towards the use of dictionaries, thesauruses and encyclopaedias written in the target language. However, if students are given too much open access to material on the web, they might find materials in the target language which are too complex, and this in turn may have a de-motivating effect. Foreign embassies, tourism offices, museums, art galleries and other cultural centre web sites are ideal starting places for background research.

On a more personal level, e-mail contact with students in other countries can offer more immediate opportunities to write for a real purpose in a foreign language, and it can occur much more frequently than the more traditional writing to a pen friend. Web-based organisations exist which put schools who are interested in such an approach in contact with one another. E-mail has the advantage of speed and also that the other person can pick up the message when it is convenient for them, meaning that time differences are not an issue.

Using video-conferencing, allowing students to talk to and see a student in another country, has even more positive motivational effects. Clearly it also allows for objects to be seen and discussed, and there are possibilities for collaborative work on text, which can be worked on by both students together. Time differences and timetables in the two schools are obstacles to this type of communication. There are also a number of 'standards' for video conferencing, with the cheaper 'Web Cam' approach (a small video camera attached to the monitor, with the data travelling over the Internet) being of the poorest quality. Higher quality equipment currently costs a great deal, and at the moment this limits the number of partner schools that you can communicate with.

The technical issues which need to be considered by MFL teachers include the connection of speakers, microphones and headphones to computers, an ability to record sound files, and an understanding of how to work with large digital, video and sound files. In particular, the transfer of large files from machine to machine requires additional storage media (such as Zip or re-writable CD-ROM drives), and the download time of some web sites, particularly those including video elements can be very long and will need to be done prior to the lesson. These technical issues are discussed in more detail in Chapter 4.

ICT also covers other technological devices with which MFL teachers will already be very familiar including telephone, fax machines and cameras (increasingly of the digital kind).

## Religious Education

This section will look at ICT activities that are appropriate specifically for religious education. Many of the activities outlined in the geography and history sections are equally appropriate for religious education.

Religious education usually focuses upon sacred texts and these can be analysed much more quickly if search facilities are used to find particular words or phrases. Where a large amount of textual material needs to be studied in some detail, it is worth introducing students to the idea of hyper-linking documents. Although hyper-linking is probably more commonly thought of as a way of linking to another web site, in order to gain more detailed information about that particular topic, it can be used within a word processed document. When students are undertaking comparative studies it is often useful to tabulate the findings so that aspects of religions can be compared more easily. At its simplest, this would involve putting data into a simple table in a word processor. The information could also be put into a well designed database if a more sophisticated solution was thought appropriate. It is very important that students realise why they are using the computer for a particular task, and when other procedures might be more appropriate. There is no point in a student reading verses from the Bible from the screen of a computer, if that is all that is being done.

The WWW contains enormous amounts of information about different religions. This gives students a wealth of information to analyse, particularly as it relates to different interpretations of religious events, but the warnings elsewhere in this book concerning validity, reliability and desirability obviously have to be heeded.

As an increasingly vast mass communications medium, the World Wide Web is the way in which ever larger numbers of people find out about religion. There are aspects of this which are clearly very beneficial, but students must also be wary of the ease with which anyone can set up a web site and disseminate their own new religion. This element of World Wide Web use is very important and we must not ignore it because we consider it dangerous or undesirable. An important part of teaching students is to ensure that their analytical powers are developed, and they are aware of the problem areas that they might encounter. The WWW does not just contain text and pictures; there are also opportunities to listen to sounds of religious significance, such as hymns and calls to prayer.

RE gives opportunities for moral dilemmas to be discussed. Simulation software which allows students to explore the range of possible consequences linked to different actions can provide an interesting structure for work of this nature. Many religious buildings will have associated web sites which will provide teachers with excellent background material to give student appropriate preparation for visits.

There are an increasing number of CD-ROM products which provide a background to different religions. These will obviously have gone through the publishing process, and their content is therefore likely to be more valid than many web sites. The costs of purchasing the CD-ROM may outweigh the time cost in searching for religious web sites which you believe to be trustworthy. Subject associations and other groups of Religious Education teachers can provide one mechanism of sharing expertise as to the usefulness of a resource. There is a tendency to see a series of RE CD-ROMs and to think that they must be purchased as they cover the area you wish students to study. You do, however, need to be aware of what advantages, if any, a CD-ROM might actually have. The medium is not the message, and in some cases the message is perhaps best shared by more traditional methods.

## Physical Education

There are no statutory requirements to work with ICT in physical education in the National Curriculum but there are many opportunities to undertake tasks using ICT.

Much can be gained by showing students moves and tactics in professional games so that they can make use of them in their own sporting activities. Currently this will involve video taping sporting events that are televised, and playing them back through a video player and television. To be most effective, great care and preparation time are needed to focus on particular elements of the event, so that time is not wasted watching elements that are not appropriate. It is rapidly becoming possible for video elements to be edited using computer software, so that only the appropriate parts are selected, and these can easily be re-run and played in slow motion, thus getting over the problems associated with the slow motion playback of video tape. We are just beginning to see the development of DVD discs which are able to hold huge amounts of video information, and which have the flexibility, using software, to control accurately the playback and speed. It is increasingly likely that teachers will not need to learn the skills necessary to make this type of compilation, as they will be soon readily available for purchase.

For a long time, videoing an individual's performance and then playing it back to them to highlight ways in which techniques could be improved have been important components of coaching. Hardware currently available, such as digital video cameras and powerful notebook computers, which are portable, now makes this realistic in a wider range of contexts. Care must obviously be taken with equipment when it is used outside, and there are important health and safety issues to consider. In many schools it might be that only in PE will students get an opportunity to work closely with video recording and playback equipment, and so PE teaching would need to develop students' ICT skills in using such equipment.

Work of this kind presumes the teacher's competence in using video and digital cameras and linking them to video playback equipment or computers. Teachers should also be aware that graphics applications need very fast processors and large amounts of memory if they are to provide clear high quality pictures. This knowledge should not be treated as complex or special, but should be compared with a modern foreign language teacher's expertise in the use of language laboratories or a physicist's use of a potentiometer.

Physiology work can well make use of CD-ROMs related to the human body, many of which utilise animations for functions of the body. A good, clear animation, projected onto a screen, or displayed on a large television screen can make complex procedures considerably easier to understand. Previously, you might have drawn a diagram onto a whiteboard or projected an image using an overhead projector, but in both cases your explanation would be linked to a basically static image. By finding an appropriate animation from a CD-ROM or a web site, your explanations can be linked to movement which will almost certainly enhance the explanation. Once you have found an appropriate animation, your preparation is reduced and the learning objectives are more likely to be achieved.

Software packages also exist that will simulate changes in the body that occur as a result of eating different kinds of food and undergoing different kinds of exercise. This type of software will appeal strongly to a generation so heavily involved in computer games, and herein lies both the advantage and disadvantage of the approach. Any type of 'game', provided appropriate feedback is given, can be 'won' by trial and error. If a student concentrates on keeping the person alive by keeping to the rules of providing appropriate nutrition and sensible exercise to the exclusion of understanding the processes that are being modelled, then the activity is a complete waste of time. Here again, it is the appropriate intervention of the teacher that is so important to the success of such an activity.

It is now possible to monitor pulse using a chest strap and a small digital heart rate monitor. Using the simpler models the data can be transferred manually from the monitor to a spreadsheet, and appropriate graphs produced. More expensive models allow the data to be directly downloaded from the monitor to the computer. It is vital in applications such as this that the technology does not get in the way of the data analysis. It would be possible for a student to go through the mechanical, technical procedure without understanding or analysing the data that is being collected. For this reason, it might be appropriate for students to go through a series of stages, so that the physical measurements are not masked by the technology.

Initially, students should attempt to measure their heart rate by taking their pulse in a traditional way, perhaps counting for 15 seconds and then multiplying by 4. Subsequently, they could use the heart monitor and relate the readings to their own degrees of exercise. The manual inputting of the data into a readily prepared spreadsheet consolidates the link between the reading on the monitor and the shape of the graph which is produced. Once the students are aware of the physical measurements that are taking place, larger number of readings and more sophisticated analysis can be undertaken using the data from the heart rate monitor downloaded directly into the computer.

Teachers will need to be able to manipulate data through the use of a database. They will need to understand the nature of the data that is being collected and the best ways of displaying it meaningfully. Many database products can very easily produce all manner of high quality charts, but many of them are meaningless. It is vital that teachers have a clear understanding of the function of such software and ways in which it can be effectively used.

Many exercise machines in fitness centres incorporate ICT in some form. However, it is important to emphasise that measuring physical quantities in their own right is not really of any use. Some exercise machines require you to enter your weight, the time for exercise and the level of exercise that you want. When you enter your weight the machine is able to approximate the amount of energy that you are using up. (Most of us will have experienced the disappointment of realising that 10 minutes of energetic exercise has only led to the loss of 10 kilocalories!) Some machines are able to add heart rate into the calculation, warning you to reduce the load as your heart rate approaches 80 per cent of its maximum. But all this data is of little use unless it can be analysed effectively, and this is where it is important to emphasise the role of teaching and coaching. Similarly, merely using video to look carefully at a student's own performance does not mean that they are able to analyse what they are doing wrong. Again the emphasis is not on replacing the teacher with ICT, but allowing the teacher to do things more effectively than he would be able to do without the technology. A coach saying what you are doing wrong is nowhere near as good as a coach showing you what you are doing wrong.

ICT can also be used productively for administrative tasks associated with PE. Sports fixtures can quickly be arranged and confirmed by e-mail rather than phone (where the other person has to be at the end of the phone at a particular time) or letter (which takes time to write and deliver). Sports fixtures can be made available on the school's Intranet, or on the school's web site if you want them accessed by a wider audience. Results and match reports can be made readily accessible to anyone, immediately, rather than posting them on a notice board, or sending them out as an announcement which is meant to be read out! The Internet also gives staff excellent opportunities to share their ideas with other colleagues nationally or internationally, through the use of basic e-mail, discussion groups or web sites.

As teachers use the World Wide Web they will quickly build up a bank of useful sites, and these can be managed effectively by putting them into named folders. The software that you use to browse the WWW will always have a facility for picking up these sites just by clicking on their saved address, rather than typing everything in again from scratch. It is quite easy to gain access to information from around the world relating to a much wider range of sports than might normally be discussed. Web sites can be found relating to every sport possible, including information from sporting organisations. Health and fitness information can also be obtained with a global perspective.

There may be times when students are required to find out information related to nutrition or health, and you might consider it appropriate for them to undertake this research using appropriate CD-ROM software or visiting a range of web sites. It is important that students are aware that while a CD-ROM has usually gone through some form of publishing process and its content is therefore likely to be truthful and reliable, web sites can be set up by anyone, and care needs to be taken as to the validity and bias of the information found on them. The most obvious example would be to check whether the information a student obtained about the dangers of smoking was from a site sponsored by Action on Smoking and Health (ASH) or by a large tobacco company.

It is possible for the teacher to store and manipulate statistics related to students' achievements in athletics, for example. This can well be stored in a spreadsheet so that simple calculations can be done automatically. For example, ranges of times can easily be equated to points scores, which can then be added up and linked to bronze, silver or gold awards. If students are expected to enter their own data into ready prepared spreadsheets, you may need to consider ways in which the data of other students can be protected, and ways in which the validity of a student's own data can also be confirmed. Protecting cells within a spreadsheet, or ensuring that data is entered into a copy of an existing spreadsheet with the original being accessed only by the teacher are approaches that could be considered.

A PE department is probably the one subject department that needs to send letters home to students frequently. The use of a word processor and a template letter can save considerable duplication of effort. Paper sheets on the sports notice board may not be the most effective medium for disseminating information to students about fixtures and sports clubs. You might want to consider integrating appropriate graphics into notices, or perhaps laying out the team members' names linked to their positions, as is often done before televised matches. Many paper-based notice boards have been replaced by more dynamic methods of displaying information. A presentation, linked to a colour monitor (or several around the school) could include a wealth of information about the PE department, including simple graphics and animation. Information on local sporting events can also be made available in order to develop students' interests in sports after they have left school.

It is acknowledged that as yet there is little material produced specifically for the use of ICT in PE. However, part of the improved network of professional discussion, through such things as the Virtual Teachers' Centre, will ensure firstly that when material does become available, it can be quickly disseminated among the PE teaching profession, but secondly that through the new swift communication channels, and through their own professional organisations, PE teachers can make known what is required to software suppliers.

It is important that you also consider where it is not appropriate to use ICT. While a carefully constructed presentation on tactics in a particular game, including animations of players moving around a pitch, interleaved with videos illustrating similar tactics being carried out both successfully and unsuccessfully in a range of first class matches, combined with a competent analysis and discussion led by an excellent teacher will have its place prior to a match, a piece of chalk and a blackboard, together with a concise 'evaluation' of the first half's play would be far more appropriate at half-time.

# CHAPTER 4

# How ICT can Enhance the Professional Role of the Teacher

## The way it could be

*On switching on your computer in the morning you are greeted with a screen containing one general e-mail relating to a change of room for the staff meeting in the afternoon, and two personal e-mails, one of which requires immediate action. You check the information required and return an e-mail to your Head of Department. You check your diary for the week on screen, and note that a meeting on the school calendar has had to be cancelled. It has been rearranged for the following week.*

*You need to arrange a meeting of the Year 8 team, so do a scheduling search, identifying when they are free to attend. The computer identifies an appropriate slot when all staff are free, so you send a message to all members of the team, asking them to confirm that they are able to attend. When all staff have confirmed, this is automatically included in their own diaries, and a message sent confirming the room for the meeting.*

*Next you need to check on some software you want to use with students in the computer room the next day. You load the software and remind yourself how to use it. You download the software activity sheet into your word processor, delete three of the available activities (the session is only 90 minutes long) and type in the session title and date in the header. You save the file and then link it to an on-screen form for print orders, selecting the number of copies and date required. You send both to the reprographics workstation.*

*You call up the list of students for your next teaching session. You get a list indicating absences from previous sessions (students use a swipe card for each session) and a note of any absences already identified by students phoning in. You enter the marks of one of your teaching groups into the appropriate section of the database.*

*You need to check on the availability and cost of some equipment you wish to order. You load the standard letter template into your word processor and type the letters. By typing in the person's name you automatically load in their address and fax number. By pressing a further key the fax is sent.*

*A small icon flashes on your screen to indicate you are receiving an e-mail document, comprising the minutes of a meeting sent to you as the chair of a local subject association committee. You check them for accuracy, make one minor addition and return them, electronically, to the secretary of the committee for distribution.*

*You belong to a special interest mailing list on teaching geography in school. You read through your special interest group e-mail messages. One correspondent points out that there is a source of copyright free photographs at the University of Buenos Aires, which it seems would make perfect illustrations for your handouts. You access the web site, look through the photos, select two, and download them onto your own disc. You then incorporate them into your handout using a desktop publishing program.*

*With the new broadband link you are able to view multimedia materials with full video and sound over the network. You contact one of the new major CD publishing houses and view ten minutes of their new multimedia program on The Weather. You are impressed with what you see and decide to use it with a group of 30 students in the Spring Term. You fill in the on-screen rental agreement and send it to the Deputy Head-Finance for authorisation, and check the availability of the multimedia computer room for the sessions. It is free, so you provisionally book the facility for five weeks. Your budget-holder spreadsheet, which you have access to at all times, is debited as the order leaves the school, and is up-dated when the final invoice arrives.*

*You decide you need a cup of coffee. You type the appropriate code and the mouse asks if you want milk and sug....*

Yes, alright, there clearly are limits to what a computer *can* do and is desirable that it *should* do. The intention of the scenario is to highlight some areas where it may actually make a significant contribution to your work by making administrative tasks quicker and more efficient, and teaching activities more motivating and productive. Everything identified in the scenario above is technologically possible. How then can we get to the position where teachers might be able to work in such a way?

## The Internet

The Internet is the infrastructure connecting computers and servers together throughout the world. Data flows around the Internet and can be received in a number of ways. The most common method is using the graphical interface known as the World Wide Web. There are a rapidly growing number of web sites which are designed to be relevant for teachers in this country.

### *The National Grid for Learning and the Virtual Teacher Centre*

These are two very important web sites which all teachers need to be familiar with.

The National Grid for Learning is effectively a gateway to other sites. The vast majority of these sites are LEA based, and many LEAs are developing web-site materials with NGfL money, some of which has to be used to develop content for the National Curriculum. There is an enormous amount of material available through this source, and it is difficult to know how teachers are expected to search through it in order to find out what might be useful. To some extent, teachers involved in the NOF ICT training initiative will be given pointers to appropriate material, but it is the intention that the material will grow rapidly, so it is difficult to keep track of developments. The danger is obviously information overload. While it is clearly sensible to give teachers opportunities to see what others are doing in other parts of the country, so that no one has to reinvent the wheel, is there much advantage in giving teachers access to 250 different types of wheel, and expecting them to find time to choose the one that best suits them?

The NGfL also has links to the Virtual Teacher Centre and to the DfEE site, important elements of which are the Schemes of Work;

the OFSTED site where all OFSTED reports are available, and to the National Curriculum web site, where all National Curriculum documentation is available in a form suitable for use with most word processors.

The Virtual Teacher Centre has a number of areas including Reception, Library, Meeting Room, Classroom Resources, School Management and Professional Development.

The Reception area provides news items and a map of the whole site. The library has web links to the UK Education Departments, Education Agencies (such as BECTa, QCA and TTA), and details of Projects and Publications. The Classroom Resources area contains a wealth of information, most of which relates to the use of ICT in curriculum subjects. The section on School Management contains government background information and links to other appropriate government agencies and suitable publications. The Professional Development section again provides information about many web sites, including a link to the General Teaching Council site.

The Meeting Room provides any teacher with the opportunity to discuss issues with their colleagues. It is worth considering this in a little more detail. There are currently two mechanisms for this communication, these being Conferences and Mailing Lists. You automatically subscribe to a mailing list (sometimes called a newsgroup) by sending by e-mail a request to join, giving your own e-mail address. This means that you really need your own personal e-mail address, rather than one which is of a generic nature. You will then receive copies of every e-mail which is sent to the mailing list, and you can respond to any you receive just by sending an e-mail to the group. On this site each mailing list is designated by a particular topic, so there is a chance that you will be interested in most of the issues raised, provided you are selective in your choice of mailing list in the first place. Remember that newsgroups are different from e-mail in that they are a completely public exchange of views.

However, there are things of which you should be aware. Firstly, suppose that you are a member of a popular mailing list. If you do not access your e-mail on a very regular basis, you will find your mailbox swamped with correspondence. You then have to spend time reading, filing and deleting a large number of messages, only a few of which may be of interest. You may not consider this a worthwhile activity. If you belong to a less popular mailing list, you might find that you get no responses to any questions which you ask and decide it is not worth subscribing to it any more.

Secondly, there are newsgroups to which, for example, mathematical problems may be sent, and on which solutions will often appear within a few hours (sometimes within minutes). Students have been known to get their coursework problems solved this way, so it is worth knowing about these groups in order to check that your tasks have not been solved by some Ph.D. student! You also need to become aware that your students may now have access to experts and knowledge that is more accurate and up-to-date than the textbooks and reference material that you have relied on for the last few years.

Conferences have a similar purpose, but work in a slightly more structured way. On the VTC they are web-based, so you have to make an active decision to log onto the web site rather than just picking up messages in your mailbox. All the contributions are 'threaded' which means that all the messages that relate to one particular topic appear together. This makes it much easier to follow logically what has been said over a period of time, and gives you an opportunity to take in all the contributions before making your own. There are, however, currently very few contributions on any of the conferences, and there are problems with such a new form of communication as the following anecdote illustrates.

On one of the threads, a participant recommended a particular web site which he thought was especially beneficial to teaching and learning in English. A representative of the DfEE, clearly pleased at such a useful contribution, replied with a message saying that this was just the sort of information which the conference should be used for. I clicked onto the hyperlink to the web site, where I was informed that publishers had complained about the inclusion of some copyright text on the web site and that because of this, the material was no longer available. One of the problems associated with publicising useful web sites!

Electronic mailing lists and conferences are still in their infancy, and they clearly offer an extremely easy way of communicating with other people. However, it is unlikely that they will be used by the vast majority of members of the teaching profession until they offer some added-value to their work. As a means of communication between a small group of people with a very specific purpose, they are excellent. Some organisations actually limit the open access use of a mailing list, preferring to sift the information and publish it weekly in an e-mail newsletter. This extra level of 'editing' ensures that the information that is received is clear, focused and reliable. The time to 'sift' through the material is committed by one person, rather than everyone doing it in their mailbox. But in a broader sense, I do not believe teachers will think it useful to spend their time disseminating information about work that they do in their school without getting something positive back.

Once all schools have access to the Internet, there is an excellent infrastructure which will enable professional information to be distributed very effectively. Currently, materials are often sent into schools, but fail, for a wide range of reasons, to actually get to the people who need to see it. Over recent years schools have been inundated with paper of all sorts, and this led to a decision at government level that most material would be of an advisory nature, and that many documents would only be sent to schools if they requested them. Sending materials electronically will actually save considerable amounts of money in postage, printing and distribution costs. If a school makes effective use of the Internet, then communication will be considerably enhanced. Interested teachers will be able to download their own copy of documentation, rather than waiting for printed copies to make their way down to them through the school hierarchy.

All school documentation will be able to be provided on the school Intranet, as will staff notices. As information about the location of new documentation is received from government agencies, this can easily be passed on to all members of staff through an on-line newsletter. Provided all staff have ready access to the Intranet, and are aware of the importance of regularly logging on to a computer, then communication within a school is likely to be considerably enhanced. Clearly, providing ease of access to information does not mean that all staff will read it, or make use of it, but it does make it possible for all staff to be kept informed relatively easily and it avoids the waste of large amounts of paper. This is not to say that electronic communication actually removes the need for paper, but it is likely that people will only go to the bother of printing out information if they are likely to make use of it.

*Subject association and other professional web sites*

Subject associations have web sites, as do the teaching unions. While originally they will have provided a relatively basic information service, increasingly, useful and relevant resource material is also being distributed through these sites. They are almost certain to have links to a wide range of other useful education sites. In some cases, the introductory pages will be open to anyone who visits, but more useful material can only be accessed if you type in a password, which you receive when you have paid your subscription!

## The implications of a school Intranet

When a school has large numbers of computers linked together on a network, and there is an ethos of open access to these computers by students, then there are opportunities for schools to develop their own Intranets, which can be used to aid the learning process.

Imagine that all your lesson learning outcomes are available to all students at all times when they access the Intranet. They can also have access to the background information which you provided them with during the lesson, and details of the questions which you set them for homework. Students who find some of the work particularly easy can be guided to extension work, or they can get hold of the details of next week's, or even next month's lessons. The very thought of giving students open access to learning resources and teaching and learning strategies immediately opens up an entirely different approach to education. What is it, for example, that you will cover in next week's lesson that is so essential that students cannot afford to miss it? Is it your enthusiastic delivery, or your carefully designed explanation of a particular process? Or, in truth, are large numbers of students in your class perfectly capable of getting on with the work without you, and is the traditional lesson structure no longer necessary if all students have access to the teaching and learning materials through the school Intranet?

These are very big issues. No longer are we just using ICT as an additional tool in order to do some things better; now we are considering how ICT could radically alter the whole approach to learning in schools. In schools that have invested heavily in ICT, one implication has been the independence with which students have been encouraged to work, particularly as to which computer programs they should use and for what purpose. The main problem in espousing such an approach is that inevitably in the beginning stages, teachers are having to undertake their traditional classroom teaching role, while at the same time, needing to develop the ICT resources for the school Intranet. In many cases, teachers have no experience of developing these kinds of resources, and this is certainly an approach which needs to be taken as part of a whole-school policy, with appropriate backing. As a professional, however, you do need to have a view on whether this is a route which is worth travelling down. With the relatively large amounts of money that Government is currently putting into ICT, the hardware and software will be there, as will the fully trained professionals. What you will need to consider is what are the advantages that might be accrued by utilising such an approach, and you should also have a clear view of the disadvantages.

## Management information systems

There are software packages designed for schools which are able to manage all of the information you are ever likely to need in the school. As an individual teacher you could keep your student records on a customised spreadsheet or database, giving you an electronic mark book. Ideally, the school's management information system could provide every individual teacher with this, keep all the data centrally and allow teachers to access it in the form most appropriate to them. This will do away with the need to keep your own incompatible data. This approach, however, needs considerable investment in software, administration and training of staff in order for it to be used effectively. It is certainly a whole-school issue.

## Strategies for supporting ICT developments in schools

A recent research report from the University of Newcastle (Moseley and Higgins 1999) has looked at how ICT can be encouraged to develop in schools. The findings show that in many classrooms, ICT is usually not linked to subject teaching or specific learning objectives in literacy and numeracy. It is far more likely to be an isolated ICT activity.

All teachers have preferred approaches to teaching, although clearly it would be expected that a range of approaches would be prevalent in most classrooms. This research suggests that more success in using ICT will be achieved if the first steps are linked to the teacher's preferred teaching style. 'For example, a teacher who favours whole-class approaches may readily adapt the use of a presentation package using a number program... with the content of the activities taught as a whole-class lesson.' (Moseley and Higgins 1999) Teachers who prefer to work with groups will find an activity involving a group of children around a computer a more comfortable start to their use of ICT. Not surprisingly then, if a teacher's first step in their use of ICT is in the pedagogic style with which they are most confident, then the ICT work is likely to be more successful and will encourage further developments.

It must be remembered that the development of ICT in schools is not the imposition of some 'new fangled ideas' which are just a high tech version of existing strategies already used successfully for many years. Indeed, if this was the case then teachers would rightly be suspicious and cynical about the large amount of money that is currently being spent on computers and training. The use of ICT in the classroom should only be considered if it enhances the educative experience which children and students receive.

The report identifies that 'issues, such as adequate access and specific technical difficulties, are real obstacles which need to be overcome if teachers are to use ICT'. This is a major problem in the development of an ICT strategy. The variations between schools as regards their number and range of computers, the software that is available, and the variability of technical support, mean that it is extremely difficult to suggest to one group of teachers in one school an approach that has worked in another school without a response such as, 'It is all very well for them, but they have got...'

So teachers in a school that has limited resources are unable to use ICT as effectively as they might like and are unable to provide a broad and balanced programme for all their students. Lack of equipment makes it difficult for staff to identify the development of their use of ICT as a priority. As ICT is not used a great deal, there is no pressure for enhancing the ICT resource from inside the school. This means that most teachers find it difficult to be aware of the possibilities. The national training (1999-2002) in the use of ICT in the classroom will attempt to open teachers' minds to the possibilities that ICT affords.

Another important finding is that ICT skills are developed more effectively during the performance of an appropriate task. Learning how to use a word processor by going through a series of irrelevant exercises is not as effective as learning the skills while producing an activity sheet for next week's lessons.

In the ICT projects which the research looked at both highly effective teachers and those identified as averagely effective obtained substantial gains in children's attainment. It was believed that these were obtained because the teachers had identified clear subject-focused objectives, they had chosen an appropriate ICT activity which could deliver those objectives, they had ascertained that the children had the appropriate ICT skills to use the computer in order to undertake the activity, and children had enough time on a computer to complete the task effectively. It is clear that the support of the head teacher or a collaborative working approach enabled the effect of the development work to be greater than had been anticipated in some institutions.

## Health and safety issues

It is important that you are aware of the health and safety issues that are relevant when using ICT equipment. This is not only for your own safety and that of the children and students with whom you are working, but additionally, it is now an element of the revised National Curriculum.

## Visual display screens

An electromagnetic field is caused by the mechanisms inside the computer's visual display unit that control the screen image. All display units are screened to prevent any damaging electromagnetic radiation being emitted but a small amount of very low frequency radiation does escape, particularly from the back of the display unit. The LCD screens on notebook computers, and the newer, flatter (and very expensive) flat screens for desktop computers, which use the same LCD technology, do not function in the same way, and electromagnetic radiation is not emitted from these types of screens. While it is very unlikely that children in school will have the opportunity to use a computer for periods long enough to be concerned about, problems like these might become issues when computer work becomes more common.

## Eyestrain and headaches

Screen glare and flickering are common causes of the eyestrain and headaches reported by those who use computers intensively. Check that the students have the brightness and contrast screen controls set to a comfortable level. Also make sure that the display unit is positioned so that the sun or overhead lights are not reflecting off the display screen. If the computer has to be used for longer periods then polarising filters that fit over the screen can be used to reduce screen glare.

## Repetitive Strain Injury (RSI)

Repetitive Strain Injury describes a range of problems characterised by pain, numbness or discomfort in the muscles, tendons, nerves and joints of the hand, wrist, forearm, elbow and upper arm, and sometimes the shoulders and neck. You need to ensure that the display screen angle and height are adjusted sensibly for each user. Position seating so that the user is comfortable and can reach all the necessary computer equipment without stretching. This can be especially problematic for primary school children who range widely in size. The ideal posture for operating a keyboard is with forearms horizontal, knees under the desk and thighs in line with the arms. The wrists should be supported by the table or a wrist rest whether using the keyboard or the mouse. Encourage students to sit upright when using the computer and, when sharing, no-one should have to twist or stretch to see the display screen.

Special concerns apply to the increasing number of students who are using laptop computers throughout the day. Laptop computers have to be compact enough to be easy to carry and so have smaller keyboards and screens making them less comfortable to use than standard sized equipment. Students using laptops should sit upright with the laptop on a firm surface at the right height for keyboarding and with the screen angled to minimise reflections. They may need to change their seating position in the class, to move away from the window for instance.

### Electrical and other hazards

Avoid overloading single sockets and make sure that leads do not trail across the floor. All food and drinks should be kept well away from the computer and other electrical equipment. This not only causes problems if crumbs get underneath the keys on the keyboard, but liquids spilled over electrical devices could be very dangerous.

Avoid carrying heavy and unwieldy computer equipment around. Instead make use of a trolley wherever possible. Special care needs to be taken when setting up temporary computer equipment in a science laboratory or an art room or even an ordinary classroom where it may take up space in which the students are used to moving around freely.

### Legal responsibilities

Teachers, like all employees, are required by law to take reasonable care of the health and safety of themselves and also of their students. You are expected to make sure that both you and the students use ICT equipment correctly and safely.

## Ethical use of software and computers

The use of computers and the ease with which information can be transferred between them has led to a variety of concerns about the legality and morality of situations that can occur, knowingly or unknowingly, with students' access to computers in schools.

## Software theft

The school ICT coordinator should make sure that the school has a licence for each copy of a program that it is running. Inform them if you have, or wish to have, a program installed. Keep an eye out for students using the school computers to distribute illegal software. Shareware should also be registered even though it might be distributed freely. However, it is common practice to allow the purchaser to keep a single copy of a program on a back-up disc in case the master disc should fail.

## Data protection and personal information

The personal data stored by schools is exempt from the Data Protection Act (1984, updated 1998) provided that it relates only to the members of the school, the data subjects have been asked whether they object to the data relating to them being held on computer and have not objected, and the data is not used for any purpose other than that for which it is held.

The Computer Misuse Act (1990) was known as the Anti-Hacking Bill and made the practice of hacking, that is breaking into others' secure computer systems, illegal. It is an offence to log onto a computer where there is no authority to do so or, if logged on legitimately to access parts of the system not covered by your authorisation. A more serious offence is committed, if in the case of the above, the motive is malicious.

## Offensive material

The Internet is unrestricted and users whether in school or at home may be exposed to unwelcome pornographic, sexist, racist and other unsuitable material both on web sites and in unsolicited e-mail. Schools can avoid accessing offensive material on the World Wide Web by signing up with an Internet Service Provider that restricts Internet access so that undesirable sites are not available to the school. Alternatively, censorship or filtering software can be installed that checks web pages and prevents them being downloaded if they contain offensive text. Downloading the desired web sites and their links to their network server's hard disc to form an Intranet rather than allowing open access to the Internet is also a possible solution.

119

In any case all schools should have an Acceptable Internet Use Policy and there should be appropriate sanctions for any student (or staff member) breaking this policy. Offensive material in e-mail is harder to control. Students' access to discussion groups and chat rooms may need to be monitored or even prevented.

### Copyright and plagiarism

The ease with which material can be 'cut and pasted' from Internet sites or CD-ROMs has led to concern over students using this material in their work without the author's permission and maybe treating it as if it were their own. An author or their publisher retains copyright over their work even when it is published on the Internet. Their permission should always be sought if it is wished to use their material as it stands.

If the material is used to support a piece of work the source should always be credited in the same way as if a book or a journal article was being used and a full reference given to enable the reader to access the original material. This is particularly important so that you can check the information source they have used. There is no guarantee that information provided by individuals on the Internet is accurate, yet many students tend to treat information from the computer as made up of unquestionable facts.

## Technical issues

While you can use a computer or other piece of technology effectively without knowing much of a technical nature, there are things which it will be increasingly important that you do know. Here is a very brief discussion of some of them, in the context of using ICT to enhance teaching and learning.

### Storing data

Data is stored in computers on discs. The most common storage medium used to be a 3¾" floppy disc. The holder is not actually very floppy, but the magnetic material inside it is. These generally hold about 1,400,000 bytes of information (1.4Mb). Roughly, you can think of 1 byte as one character in a document or 1 pixel in a digital photograph. So one floppy disc can hold quite a lot of text documents, but not many photographs.

Most computers will now have a hard disc inside them. This is where all your programs are stored, and it is increasingly where you will save your text documents and digital photographs while you are working with them. Because hard disc drives are able to hold very large amounts of information (the one in my notebook computer is 8 Gigabytes – that is 8,000,000,000 bytes) it is easy to forget how large a file might be. It only becomes a problem if you want to move the file from your computer and give it to someone else who will want to use it on their own computer.

If you save your work to a floppy disc, the biggest file you can move is 1.4 Mbytes. Give your floppy disc to your colleague and they will be able to load the file into their own computer, and provided that they have the program that was used to produce it, then they will be able to see (or hear) it. There are other storage devices which are able to hold much larger files. Zip discs are able to hold 100 Mb or 250 Mb, but they need a separate Zip drive attached to your computer. It is also possible to save data onto writable or re-writable CD-ROMs, although again you need an extra piece of hardware attached to your computer. A CD-ROM can hold 600Mb. If your computer has a CD-ROM drive then it can read CD-ROMs produced by a CD-ROM writer, but an ordinary CD-ROM drive cannot create new CD-ROM discs.

If your computer is linked to the Internet, then you will be able to attach the file you want to move to an e-mail and send it to your colleague electronically. Very big files can be moved in this way, but it can take a long time, particularly if your Internet connection is through an ordinary telephone line. Much software, particularly upgrades and sampler material, is distributed over the Internet in this way.

*Connecting computers in networks*

If you want to send a large file to a colleague in your own school, and you have a network installed, then that should be your preferred method of distribution. Computers on a network are all connected to a relatively powerful computer called a server. The server has a very large hard disc, and all the software and all the text, data and graphics files could be stored on this disc. When you sit at a network computer and load a word processing package into your machine, the software could be downloading from the server rather than from the hard disc on your own machine. This approach has both advantages and disadvantages.

In administrative terms, you only need to install a piece of software once (on the server) rather than on every individual computer. The machines do not have to have their own hard discs, meaning that they can be cheaper, and students' and teachers' work can be stored on one server hard disc, which means that you do not have to go back to the same machine every time to find your files. It also means that one printer and one scanner could be connected to the network, which everyone could have use of.

However, the programs often load much more slowly from the server, as the data has to flow down the cables from the main hard disc, and this can be frustrating particularly when a group of students all need to load the same program at the same time. This problem can be alleviated to some extent by loading the most frequently used programs onto each computer and only accessing the more unusual ones from the server. As the speed with which data can travel from server to computer increases due to technological advances, the need to have a highly intelligent computer at every network point is removed. By using less sophisticated and cheaper 'network' computers attached to one very sophisticated server with cabling which will allow for very swift movement of data, you can get the best of both worlds, and this is the direction in which many people believe computing in schools could go.

When your students start working with more sophisticated programs they are likely to be creating much bigger files than they did previously. This is when you need to be aware of the issues discussed above.

### Processors and random access memory (RAM)

A processor is the heart of the computer. Generally, the higher the specification of the processor, the faster programs will load, and the more quickly they will react.

When you start a program (click on a word processor icon, for example) the program data is copied from the hard disc into random access memory (RAM). All the time you are using the program, the changes are taking place in this memory chip. If you were to have a sudden power cut, all the data in the memory chip would be lost, but a copy of the program would still be there on the hard disc. If you remembered to save your document or graphic file onto the hard disc, you would be able to retrieve your work. If you did not, then all the work you did would be lost. It is very important that you save your work at regular intervals (at least every ten minutes) so that you never lose hours of work.

Many of the sophisticated things you can do with computer programs arise because you are able to have a number of programs running at the same time. You can, for example, copy someone's name and address out of your address list, and paste it into a letter in your word processor. You need a lot of RAM in order to run a number of programs at the same time, and if you have not got enough, programs run very slowly, which can be frustrating. A typical computer will have 64 Mbytes of RAM or more.

## Connecting peripherals to your computer

At the back of many computers there is a bewildering array of different shaped sockets and connectors, with a multitude of wires leading from the computer to other pieces of hardware. Typically, you will have a power lead, a mouse, a monitor and a printer connected. You are also increasingly likely to have leads from a modem or network card. A modem converts digital data from the computer into analogue data which can be sent down the telephone line, and reverses the process when you are receiving data from the Internet. This may well be the set up you have at home. A network card is the piece of electronics which connects your computer to a server as part of a network. In this case all the data remains in a digital form. This is likely to be the way your computers at school will be operating.

Increasingly, computers are being fitted with USB ports. The big advantages of this are that peripherals can be connected and disconnected without having to restart your computer, the speed of data transfer is relatively fast, and in most cases the power to the peripheral is provided down the USB cable via the computer, which means that you will not have to have a separate power supply for every extra piece of hardware you want to use. Many computers have infra-red ports which allow communication, say between your computer and a suitable printer, to be undertaken without any connecting leads at all, using similar technology to a TV remote handset. Some schools are also experimenting with totally wireless networks, using radio links between portable computers and the network hardware.

As ICT develops, and these technologies become more prevalent and more reasonably priced, you will have the opportunity to decide how you can use the facilities to best enhance the teaching and learning of your students.

### Backing-up data

Electronic data stored on a hard disc is very vulnerable. If, for example, a fault developed on your hard disc drive, and you were unable to access anything on it, how much work would you have lost? The legitimate software you will have purchased can relatively easily be reinstalled from your own CD-ROMs or floppy discs, but what about your own worksheets, your reports, your departmental finance spreadsheets, your digital photographs, your sound files, the important e-mail messages, the list of your favourite web sites and perhaps the novel you have been working on?

In truth, because a hard disc can hold so much information, we probably do save more than we actually need, and often the time taken to open old files to see if they might be useful one day, and then to delete them, seems excessive. But on a hard disc that is clearly structured, with named folders and sensible clear file names, there will be a great deal of information that you would not want to lose, and the only way you can be certain that you will not lose it is by producing a copy of all your files which you can store well away from your own computer. It is probably unrealistic to expect a carefully structured daily back-up procedure for your own personal or departmental computers, although this should certainly be considered for school networks. But it is really important that you have somewhere a copy of all the files that you have created (and are therefore important to you), probably on a re-writable CD-ROM or on a Zip drive.

## Notebook and palmtop computers

Although more expensive than desktop computers, small notebook computers are now available that have tremendous power. There are government backed schemes which are encouraging teachers and head teachers to use notebook computers for all elements of their work. In one relatively portable package you have a colour screen integrated into the lid, large capacity hard discs, fast processors, large amounts of RAM, a modem or network card, CD-ROM or even a DVD drive and stereo speakers. Being portable means that you will carry it around, and you should always have the files on it that you need – they will never be 'on your other computer at home'. A modem will allow you to pick up any e-mail you might have from any location with a telephone, and similarly you will be able to log onto the World Wide Web. Trials of using notebook computers with students have also been most successful, and as the cost of this type of machine continues to drop, it will not be long before it will be feasible, and perhaps desirable, for every student in a school to have their own.

Palmtop computers are much smaller than notebooks, and, because of their size, the facilities they offer are rather limited. Generally, material can be downloaded onto desktop machines, but some procedures need to be gone through to ensure the file formats are compatible. Because of their small sizes, the keyboards are inevitably small, so typing can be rather slow. Many palmtops can enter data by writing on the screen with a stylus, and the software translates the writing into typed text.

## Anti-viral software

The problem started when some programmers decided to design a program that would cause irreparable harm to someone else's computer! These viruses, as they were soon to be called, were spread from machine to machine by floppy disc. Once the virus is actually on the machine, it can then just sit there, if you are lucky, or it can make substantive changes to material on your hard disc. In the days of stand alone machines, careful checking of the floppy disc with a virus checker program would ensure that nothing untoward arrived on your machine. Now that computers are almost always linked together, and that one of the main purposes is to communicate and transfer information and programs, this inevitably means that viruses can now very easily end up on your machine.

There are estimated to be 45,000 different viruses, and removing them from your machine does not mean that they are destroyed forever. It is therefore essential that you have an efficient anti-virus strategy if you want to avoid potential catastrophe ( all your student mark data being destroyed for example). Having a piece of anti-virus software on all of your machines is therefore essential, but you must also consider how the database of potential viruses is to be kept right up-to-date. Running an out-of-date piece of anti-virus software can give you a sense of false security. The program says that none of your files are infected, but it is only aware of viruses that existed up to six months ago. This is particularly true of trial anti-virus software which you might download from a web site or from a magazine cover CD-ROM. Check how old the database of viruses is which the program uses.

Viruses are programs, and therefore cannot be distributed through data itself. So the text of an e-mail message cannot spread a virus, but an attachment to an e-mail, which might be a program, could. Similarly, the text in a word processed document, the figures in a spreadsheet or the graphics in a paint package cannot spread viruses, but unfortunately, the macros, or small automated elements in these type of packages, are programs and therefore can spread viruses. Sometimes the infection will cause annoyance, but it could cause you to lose weeks, months or years of valuable work.

## Hoax viruses

As soon as you have access to e-mail you will receive messages from friends and colleagues passing on information about the latest virus. In the majority of cases this will be an example of a hoax virus. Hoax viruses will cause no damage to your system, but they will have achieved their writer's aim of being distributed widely throughout the world. They are the electronic version of the chain letter, and should be dealt with in a very similar way.

## Looking to the future

In writing this book I have attempted to give a very general overview of the ways in which ICT can be used to enhance teaching and learning in schools. In doing so I have attempted to address situations varying from one where a classroom has one computer in the corner to one where all students throughout the school have their own notebook computer. In many cases the actual activity and the learning associated with it are no different. The difference comes in the management of the resources. I hope, however, that no one reading this book will feel that 'There are some good ideas here, but it will never work in this school because we do not have sufficient equipment'. Make use of what ICT resources you have, and see how it can enhance what you are doing in school. When you are convinced, argue your case for more ICT equipment from a position of knowledge and conviction. As a professional, you now know what can be achieved, and what you need to be able to do better.

Instead of buying existing software and seeing how it will fit into the curriculum you want to deliver, tell the software houses and the large number of ICT content providers who are putting material onto the National Grid for Learning what *you* need in order to make your teaching more effective. And the mechanism for you to do that is already in place. Interactive discussion groups as part of the Virtual Teacher Centre or discussion groups set up by your own subject associations provide the ideal medium for this type of debate.

My intention was not only to provide you with some ideas as to how you can better integrate ICT into your lessons so that the teaching and learning in your classroom becomes more effective today, but also to provide you with an embryonic vision of how you might make the best use of the ICT facilities which you will undoubtedly encounter tomorrow.

# References

Ager, R. (1998) *Information and Communications Technology in Primary Schools: Children or Computers in Control?* London: David Fulton Publishers.

Covey, S. R. (1989) *The Seven Habits of Highly Effective People.* London: Simon and Schuster.

Gardner, H. (1993) *Frames of Mind: The Theory of Multiple Intelligence.* London: Fontana Press.

Moseley, D. and Higgins, S. (1999) *Ways Forward with ICT: Effective Pedagogy using ICT for Literacy and Numeracy in Primary Schools.* Newcastle: University of Newcastle.

Somekh, B. (1997) 'Classroom investigations: exploring and evaluating how IT can support learning' in Somekh, B. and Davis, N. (eds) *Using Information Technology Effectively in Teaching and Learning*, 114–126. London: Routledge.

Stevenson, D. (1997) *Information and Communications Technology in UK Schools: An Independent Inquiry.* London: The Independent ICT in Schools Commission.

Underwood, J. and Brown, J. (eds) (1997) *Integrated Learning Systems: Potential into Practice.* Oxford: Heinemann.

Vygotsky, L. S. (1978) *Mind in Society: The Development of Higher Psychological Processes.* Cambridge, USA: Harvard University Press.

# Index

Printed in the United Kingdom
by Lightning Source UK Ltd.
104595UKS00001BA/7-9